MW00834986

MARY CRUSHES THE SERPENT

30 YEARS' EXPERIENCES OF AN EXORCIST
TOLD IN HIS OWN WORDS

Written by an Exorcist Priest
Edited by Fr. Theodore Geiger, 1934
Translated by Fr. Celestine Kapsner, OSB

AND

BEGONE SATAN !

A SOUL-STIRRING ACCOUNT OF DIABOLICAL
POSSESSION IN IOWA

Written by Fr. Carl Vogl
Translated by Fr. Celestine Kapsner, OSB, 1923

Caritas Publishing

Previously published in the early 1900's, these two books, *Mary Crushes the Serpent* and *Begone Satan!* have been retypeset and are presented together in this one volume, published in honor of Our Lady, June 4, 2016, the Feast of the Immaculate Heart of Mary.

The exorcist-author of the first book was a religious priest ordered by his bishop to set forth in writing his decades-long experiences as an exorcist. The editor, Fr. Gieger, kept his name secret, but recounts that he was reputed for his priestly zeal and untiring and heroic sacrifices. He died in 1909, at the age of seventy-seven, remembered and honored as a saintly man.

Fr. Theophilus Riesinger (1868 - 1941), the exorcist of the second book, was ordained a priest in 1899. He was a Capuchin Franciscan. Although he was born in Germany, he later resided in Marathon, Wisconsin, in the United States, and perfomed the exorcism of *Begone Satan!* in Iowa. Fr. Carl Vogl authored the account of that exorcism.

Fr. Celestine Kapsner (1892 - 1973), was a Benedictine monk of St. John's Abbey at Collegeville, Minnesota, and translated both books into English.

ISBN: Paperback: 978-1-945275-03-6
ISBN: Hardback: 978-1-945275-04-3

Library of Congress Control Number: 2016946383

For our fight is not with human enemies,
but with the principalities and powers
who originate the darkness in this world,
the spiritual army of evil in the heavens.

(Eph 6:12)

Remember, when we jeer at the devil and tell ourselves
that he does not exist, that is when he is happiest.

Fr. Gabriel Amorth, Exorcist

President, International Association of Exorcists

CONCERNING THE DEVIL AND DEMONS

Behind the disobedient choice of our first parents lurks a seductive voice, opposed to God, which makes them fall into death out of envy.[266] Scripture and the Church's Tradition see in this being a fallen angel, called "Satan" or the "devil".[267] The Church teaches that Satan was at first a good angel, made by God: "The devil and the other demons were indeed created naturally good by God, but they became evil by their own doing."[268]

Scripture speaks of a sin of these angels.[269] This "fall" consists in the free choice of these created spirits, who radically and irrevocably rejected God and his reign. We find a reflection of that rebellion in the tempter's words to our first parents: "You will be like God."[270] The devil "has sinned from the beginning"; he is "a liar and the father of lies".[271]

It is the irrevocable character of their choice, and not a defect in the infinite divine mercy, that makes the angels' sin unforgivable. "There is no repentance for the angels after their fall, just as there is no repentance for men after death."[272]

Scripture witnesses to the disastrous influence of the one Jesus calls "a murderer from the beginning", who would even try to divert Jesus from the mission received from his Father.[273] "The reason the Son of God appeared was to destroy the works of the devil."[274] In its consequences the gravest of these works was the mendacious seduction that led man to disobey God.

The power of Satan is, nonetheless, not infinite. He is only a creature, powerful from the fact that he is pure spirit, but still a creature. He cannot prevent the building up of God's reign. Although Satan may act in the world out of hatred for God and his kingdom in Christ Jesus, and although his action may cause grave injuries - of a spiritual nature and, indirectly, even of a physical nature - to each man and to society, the action is permitted by divine providence which with strength and gentleness guides human and cosmic history. It is a great mystery that providence should permit diabolical activity, but "we know that in everything God works for good with those who love him."[275]...

When the Church asks publicly and authoritatively in the name of Jesus Christ that a person or object be protected against the power of the Evil One and withdrawn from his dominion, it is called exorcism. Jesus performed exorcisms and from him the Church has received the power and office of exorcizing.[176] In a simple form, exorcism is performed at the celebration of Baptism. The solemn exorcism, called "a major exorcism," can be performed only by a priest and with the permission of the bishop. The priest must proceed with prudence, strictly observing the rules established by the Church. Exorcism is directed at the expulsion of demons or to the liberation from demonic possession through the spiritual authority which Jesus entrusted to his Church. Illness, especially psychological illness, is a very different matter; treating this is the concern of medical science. Therefore, before an exorcism is performed, it is important to ascertain that one is dealing with the presence of the Evil One, and not an illness.[177]

~ *Catechism of the Catholic Church 391-395, 1673*

[266] Cf. Gen 3:1-5; Wis 2:24. [267] Cf Jn 8:44; Rev 12:9. [268] Lateran Council IV (1215): Denzinger-Schonmetzer, *Enchiridion Symbolorum, definitionum et declarationum de rebus fidei et morum* (1965) 800. [269] Cf. 2 Pt 2:4. [270] Gen 3:5. [271] I Jn 3:8; Jn 8:44. [272] St. John Damascene, Defide orth. 2, 4: PG 94, 877. [273] Jn 8:44; cf. Mt 4:1-11. [274] I Jn 3:8. 275 Rom 8:28. [176] Cf. Mk 1:25-26; 3:15; 6:7, 13; 16:17. [177] Cf. Codex Iuris Canonici, can. 1172.

CONTENTS

MARY CRUSHES THE SERPENT

BEGONE SATAN !

Mary Crushes the Serpent

The Serpent

30 Years' Experiences of an Exorcist
Told in His Own Words

Sequel to Begone Satan !

Written by an Exorcist Priest
Edited by Fr. Theodore Geiger, 1934
Translated by Fr. Celestine Kapsner, OSB

PREFACE

It seems providential that an interesting work written by a religious giving his experiences as an exorcist came into my hands not long ago. He was entrusted with this office by the bishop of a large non-German diocese wherein he carried on his duties constantly for a period of more than thirty years. This treatise is very instructive and will certainly prove helpful to many, especially to those in charge of souls. It will enlighten and clarify them in distinguishing spirits of different origin, as well as enable them to see the providence of God far better.

The extraordinary phenomena of preternatural practices, divine as well as diabolical, that have become more common in our day cannot escape our attention. The enlightened who still maintain that the powers of nature are unlimited are thus put on their mettle by these positive facts of the preternatural. Hence it is but proper to make the rich experiences of this religious more widely known. I will keep secret his name as well as the names of all others mentioned therein so to embarrass no one. However, I will say that he was a talented person, versed in mathematical and theological studies, and reputed for his priestly zeal and untiring and heroic sacrifices. He died in 1909, at the age of seventy-seven, remembered and honored as a saintly man. His religious superiors placed this inscription above his resting place: "His life as a religious was exemplary, filled with discretion and worthy of esteem. Whenever a naturally disagreeable task was to be done, such as taking care of the sick at night, or replacing a sick or incapacitated confrere, he was always obliging. Thus he spent days hearing confession in different languages. He practiced penance in a high degree for many years by spending his sleeping hours in an ordinary straight chair instead of resting his body on a soft bed. His jovial disposition towards his associates led no one to suspect him of leading such a virtuous life. Smilingly he accepted jocular remarks about himself though they were at times unpleasant to him, sometimes even very stinging. He enjoyed robust health nearly all of his life having little need for the services of physician or dentist.

"His appointment to the office of exorcist in 1878 brought him enemies from many quarters. We need not be surprised that he was ridiculed by some. But during his thirty years of labor he has brought help and relief to a great many of the possessed and obsessed. The courage with which he subdued Satan and the authority with which he was capable of commanding the dragon are convincing proof of the saintliness of his life.

"In spite of ill health during the fall of 1909, he was called away on a journey to conduct an exorcism. The following day, however, becoming mortally ill he was brought back home to die a peaceful death on November 5 at eight in the morning."

A priest of such far reaching experience and so highly regarded by his superiors is certainly a trustworthy witness to the truth and not a mere credulous observer and reporter. At the demand of the diocesan bishop he recorded his experiences, to which he refers as his "records". His annotations seem to me to be of special importance in order to give a true interpretation to the author.

"Your Excellency! In obedience to your repeated requests I have written down the records so desired by you. I should have handed them over to you long ago, but as I am not skilled in the art of writing, I could never be satisfied with my composition. I did not consider it fit to be submitted to you although I tried to rewrite it repeatedly.

"The object of this document is to show the maternal solicitude of the Blessed Virgin for the Church of her Divine Son, as also to publish the plan Mary seems to have adopted to come to the aid of the Church in her present plight.

"I have prayed to the Blessed Virgin to guide my hand that my work may help to give honor to the Mother of Mercy and to reveal and esteem the inexhaustible goodness of her heart. It is of itself evident that I submit these records and their contents in advance to the judgment of Holy Mother Church."

The bishop submitted the records to the Holy Office at Rome. The author was informed by the Holy Office that the work was highly praiseworthy and that it contained nothing contrary to the teachings of the Church. They called his attention especially to the fact that his entire work harmonized with the considerations which at that very time moved the Holy Father, Pope Leo XIII, to compose the prayer to be said after Mass in order to counteract the attacks of Satan.

These intrigues of Satan are not less active today than they were 30 years ago. Hence this treatise should interest people as much now as it did then.

The reader, must ever keep in mind that the following records are not my own experiences. It is not I, but rather the anonymous author that speaks. I am giving his records word for word translated from a foreign language without any alteration. I tried to make certain details clearer, some objectionable features I expunged. My own remarks are at the beginning of each chapter as also the preface and conclusion.

The first chapter deals with possession in general and its characteristic marks. The second tells of certain confessions made by the demons. The third gives the confirmation from heaven of what the demons confessed to be true.

May it all serve for the greater honor of God, to the glory of the Son of God, Jesus Christ, the Victor over death and hell, and may it also contribute to the honor of the Blessed Mother, who crushes the head of the serpent.

REV. THEODORE GEIGER, 1934,
Cathedral Rector, Bamberg.

PART I

POSSESSION AND ITS MEANING

It was about the time of Easter in 1874 that I began to function as an exorcist. I accepted my first case only under obedience, and not because I sought this type of work. Since then, now nearly 26 years ago, I was constantly engaged in this burdensome yet consoling and instructive occupation.

I have pronounced the rites of exorcism over a great many possessed men and women, mostly the latter. Some of these had caused their own unfortunate condition. Others came under the influence of Satan through no fault of their own, but because of curses pronounced against them. Still others of the possessed were, I found, especially select souls which God had called to, and prepared for, a high state of perfection. We have had saints at all times who were subject not only to the ordinary temptations of the evil one, but who had to submit to ordeals which cannot be explained by any laws of nature. Yet in the midst of the most terrible attacks these saints retained their personal freedom and self-mastery. The devil tortured them without having them in his possession. This is called obsession, that is, control from without.

The possessed person is no longer himself, as the adjective itself already suggests. He loses the voluntariness to act freely of himself, because his actions and thoughts occur by the power of the demon that possesses him. The demon exercises an inner force over the bodily organs and the sensible functions of the possessed and in that way forces his victim to think, speak, feel and act according to the whims of the devil possessing him. For example, should the possessed like to say a prayer, the devil immediately causes him to utter blasphemies instead of prayers.

I was once visited by a possessed woman who came out of politeness but who throughout her stay reprimanded and spoke unbecoming things to me. Finally the demon himself made his appearance and told me: "She came with the intention of speaking becomingly to you, but she did not count on her master being with her. She is really sorry for her insulting remarks but she will tell you more." In fact, the poor creature lamented such unbecoming remarks in my presence, nevertheless she continued to carry on in the same manner.

Another sure sign of possession is the presence of a twofold reaction. They are easily distinguishable from each other by their opposite effects. One should rather say that there are two distinct interchangeable personalities. The one person thinks, speaks and acts just the opposite of what the other person thinks, speaks and acts. One person that was gentle, obedient, reverent, pious, and meek by her very nature is suddenly changed to the very opposite and becomes indecent, godless and vile in her speech, rude and stubborn in her conduct. Should someone then make a remark about her behavior or contradict her, she would break out in menacing anger regardless of who was present. She would threaten her opponent with physical violence accompanied with caustic remarks.

Good people with a vacillating nature are not uncommon. Hence one should not be surprised to come in contact with some who are at times very good and yet may become very ill-mannered. This unsteadiness is due to the natural dispositions of such persons. But when you notice the highest degree of opposite characteristics in the same person, as in the case of one who, although naturally very well disposed, pious, zealous in doing good, suddenly reveals the opposites of these virtues, you are tempted to say: "She is not herself. She herself would not speak nor act in such a manner." If one should find in place of the above named virtues, a wicked disposition, godlessness, hatred, madness, and all of these displayed in the highest degree in a person, one can rightly fear and suspect that the person is possessed. I will mention just one case from actual experience.

I was called to a certain home to which the mother had previously brought a statue of a saint to be used as an ornament in a room. At the sight of this statue the daughter became raving mad and, taking a hammer, pounded it into pieces. This action together with previous manifestations of the sort puzzled me and I was tempted to say to her: "Either you are crazy or you are possessed." One day I was inclined to speak the short form of exorcism over her without telling her what I was doing. After giving her absolution in confession I said a few words in Latin against the demon. Suddenly the girl became unconscious and the demon betrayed himself. Upon my request he answered that there were three demons in her Bel, Beelzebub, and Cerberus.

An aversion for holy things is a further sign of possession. The possessed will notice within himself a constant disposition against all prayer and frequently will be incapable of praying at all. He feels a dislike towards all pious practices. The sight of a devout picture annoys him. He feels tempted to contradict the preachers in the pulpit. His presence in church, especially at Holy Mass, is tedious to him, and sometimes he leaves the church suddenly without knowing the reason why. All this resistance, disturbance, and annoyance is brought on by the demon possessing the person and anything that pertains to God and religion causes him intense pain. And because he smarts under these circumstances the demon causes the possessed person to turn indeliberately away from all holy things.

When one forces the possessed to do that which he hates to do, the demon is tortured to such an extent that, having lost his self-control, he blurts out and betrays himself. This has been a frequent experience of mine. Here is an example. While talking with a possessed person I purposely turned the conversation to matters of no consequence. The possessed remained quiet. Then I purposely spoke about God and the soul. The demon made himself known at once. I directed the conversation again to ordinary things and he immediately retired. This test was repeated a number of times, always with the same results. At another time the demon said: "You can speak to me about anything you wish and I will permit you to speak, but when you introduce God into your conversation I will be on the spot at once." He kept his word.

The characteristic marks that I have mentioned are the ordinary signs of possession. Should you find them present in a person, you can fairly presume that there is a real case of possession at hand. However, the most powerful means to assure oneself of what to expect in the possessed is the exorcism itself. Exorcism forces the demon to make himself known.

The soul of the possessed, so to say, retreats within himself. The demon has control over the person's bodily senses and organs and uses them as instruments for his own speech and acts. The body of the possessed becomes the property of the demon who has possession of it throughout the course of the exorcism. The possessed no longer has any sense perception. The bodily impressions no longer have any influence upon the senses. The natural consciousness disappears al-together. This, however is superseded by a supernatural diabolical perceptiveness caused by the presence of the demon in the body of the possessed whose senses are controlled by the demon instead of by the soul.

You can shout into the ears of the possessed, you can open his eyes by force and place an article before him to see, you can pinch him, prick him with needles, but the possessed is not conscious of anything you do.

On the other hand as soon as you pronounce the holy name of Jesus, or say a part of a prayer, or place a crucifix on the eyes of the possessed, or show him a holy picture; or if the priest touches him with his anointed hands, or with the stole, a painful movement is at once noticeable upon the body of the possessed, frequently accompanied with forceful contortions, gnashing of teeth or screams. These are marks of diabolical sensibility which have suppressed the natural sensibility. These manifestations also indicate the pain which the demon is suffering. The touch, the sight, merely the presence of anything blessed, holy or consecrated to God causes the demon terrible pains. One can see what an abhorrence the demon has for all holy things especially during the process of exorcism. He will break and tear the thing into pieces should he succeed in getting hold of it.

As soon as the demon appears, he addresses everyone in the second person. It is readily seen that another person has taken the place of the possessed and that another self besides that of the possessed is in control. This being speaks about itself in the first person and of the possessed in the third person, for example: "I will make her suffer." "You will not escape me." This being maintains to be the demon himself and not the person whose body he controls.

Whenever the demon fails to give his name of his own accord, the exorcism can force it out of him. During the course of years in which I conducted many exorcisms I came across all the names of the demons mentioned in Holy Scripture, also the names of the heathen gods and goddesses. All the demons submitted their names and were made helpless after a longer or shorter battle. In most instances the names of the demons were unknown to the possessed, in fact, the latter had never heard of them.

Many of the demons that appeared to test their power, assumed names of persons noted in history for the harm they have done to the Church and to souls through their teaching, their crimes, or their cruelty. Some of them were unknown to me, and I had to make use of a historical dictionary to acquaint myself with the persons whose names the demons had taken.

It seems they have a predelection for such names or persons through whom they have evidently and successfully injured the Church. In this they imitate generals of war who often bear the name of the battles wherein they gained their decisive and glorious victory. There is a demon by the name of Judas, a demon by the name of Elizabeth of England, a demon by the name of Voltaire... very likely they are the demons who succeeded in harming the Church through these historical characters.

I do not wish to imply by these statements that I am making a general rule. One can also advance a different interpretation. All I wish to do is to present the facts that manifested themselves in the course of the battles of these victim souls. The names of all the great opponents and persecutors of the Church from the time of King Herod to the present were mentioned during these ordeals and they were defeated under the name each had chosen.

During my first three years of exorcising I was occupied chiefly with three possessed persons. These showed the usual marks of genuine diabolical possession. To convince me more positively and to instruct me better, God undoubtedly permitted the demon to give very extraordinary signs of his presence and powers so as to give evident proofs that these persons were really possessed. I will mention a few of these manifestations.

In the recreation room of a cloister, where I conducted an exorcism, a statue of the Blessed Virgin stood in a glass bell mid-high upon a pedestal attached to one of the four walls. In the same room to the right adjoining wall there was a canopy. Towards the end of the exorcism the possessed was reclining upon the carpet on the floor. The demon was on the point of leaving. I commanded him to leave a sign of his departure. The Roman ritual confers this power upon the exorcist. At the same time I indicated to him what sign I wanted. As a sign of his departure I demanded him to break one of the panes in the glass door of the room. The demon at first hesitated to give this signal, but I insisted upon it. Suddenly those who were with me heard the noise of a window crash coming from where the canopy hung. We turned around facing the canopy to see what had happened. This is what we saw. An invisible hand had taken the glass bell containing the statue of the Blessed Virgin from the pedestal and placed it in the farthest corner of the canopy. The panes of glass covering the statue were all separated but none were broken. They were, lying beside the statue, undamaged.

There is no natural explanation for such an incident. Had the statue dropped of itself it would have fallen perpendicularly and would have been lying along the foot of the wall where the pedestal was still attached. In no case could it have fallen into the corner of the canopy which was diagonally situated about 1 to 70 degrees, from the pedestal. The statue evidently was carried by an invisible hand from the pedestal to the corner of the canopy. The demon gave this signal in place of the one I had asked for.

On numerous occasions I have commanded the demons to impress a mark upon the body of the possessed. They obeyed this command more than thirty times, and in every case the impress was left by an invisible hand. I told them to place the names, of Jesus, Mary, the Sacred Heart, and of Pius IX upon the arm or above the breast of the possessed. At the close of the exorcism all present could see the names impressed just as I had ordered. These marks were perfectly imprinted, cut through the skin deep into the living flesh somewhat like the branding of cattle. These scars of the branding remain to this day. I always demanded that these marks be placed upon the arm or above the breast so that I could easily and properly see them with my own eyes. On the feast of the Immaculate Conception, in 1878, I made an exception and in the Latin tongue purposely ordered the demon to brand the name of Jesus upon the back of the possessed. After the exorcism and before the other attendants had departed, we bared the back of the possessed and found thereon the monogram of Jesus cut deep into the flesh, even the three nails appeared underneath.

On one occasion as one of the possessed was delivered from a demon we demanded that she hang a heart as an offering under the statue of the Blessed Virgin mentioned above as standing upon the pedestal. She consented. We suggested that she place a strip of paper with her name upon it into the heart. She carried out this suggestion to the letter.

During one of the following exorcisms the demon made known to me that he had a document in his possession which the possessed handed over to him twenty-three years ago when she was but eleven years old. This document, signed with her own blood contained her willingness to hand herself over to the demon. I ordered the demon to surrender this note to me. Suddenly he yelled out with a strong commanding voice: "Take it away!" Then he said: "I am not speaking to you but to my own." Then he added with a sign of satisfaction: "Look into the heart and see if the name (of the possessed) is still there." We opened the heart and in amazement found that the name was no longer there. The demon had it removed by one of his servants. I remonstrated: "How dare you remove what has been dedicated to the Blessed Virgin?" The demon answered: "The Virgin did not accept it because the possessed did not do it with a sincere intention, but my note she has given to me with a sincere heart."

I considered it very important to deprive the demon of that unfortunate note and so I insisted upon his returning it. Towards the end of one of the following exorcisms the demon was filled with trembling and fear. He fell upon his knees and said with a quivering voice that the Blessed Virgin was present. Immediately he turned his head towards an invisible person and said: "Where shall I place it?"

A moment later he said to me: "I am leaving, and I will pass through the chapel and will put everything at the feet of the statue of Joseph. But handle the note carefully because it has passed through the fire of hell." And the demon passed out. All of us went to the chapel and really found a paper folded together like an envelope in front of the statue of St. Joseph. It had a yellow color, was dirty and emitted a very disgusting odor. I unwrapped the paper and found that it contained two notes. The one the demon had taken from the votive stand and the other, namely, the document of twenty-three years ago with the written agreement still upon it.

The possessed recognized this document written by her at the age of eleven. She turned frightfully pale. The date of the note and the name of the possessed were written upon the document in her own blood. The demon on his part had signed his name underneath on both of the notes. He signed himself, "Bel".

Now I understood why the demon had said: "I will place everything there." The Blessed Virgin had forced him to return not only the document, but also the note with the name which he stole from the votive stand. I also understood now why the demon had said: "Take hold of it carefully for it went through the fire of hell." In fact the document was very brittle and on the point of crumbling to pieces as if it had been exposed to a strong fire. Here there could have been no deception. Such facts as these could not be explained in natural terms.

The possessed woman travelled a great distance to come to the main city for exorcism. She did not go through the chapel but came directly to me in the recreation room where we were awaiting her and where the exorcism took place. From our position we could see her enter the main gate and come directly to the recreation room situated opposite the gate. After her entrance she was never alone as I and the witnesses of the exorcism were constantly with her.

I had mentioned that the demon, Bel, had signed his own name to both notes which he returned. The same demon also wrote his name on the wall of the room in which the exorcism took place. He wrote with an invisible hand in the presence of the witnesses of the exorcism. During the exorcism the demon Zachar wrote his name on the wall: "I am Zachar, I have tortured P. Surin, and I will leave on the ninth of September."

Lucifer himself was forced to write the name of Pius IX on the painting: "I am leaving, disgracefully banished through the Virgin. Lucifer." I valued this writing of the Chief of hell so highly that I sent it to a holy place of pilgrimage.

Once the demon told me about an affair that was going on at the same time some seventy miles away from my residence. I took notice of what the demon had said, had it signed by witnesses present, and sent it to the pastor of the place for verification. His reply assured me that everything had happened just as the demon had indicated.

At another time the demon informed me what was going on at the same time about thirty miles away. I investigated the matter myself, and can vouch for the actual facts. Things about myself as well as matters concerning other persons about which the possessed could neither have been a witness nor could have known the least thing were also mentioned by the demon.

Whenever the demons began to gesticulate fiercely, I begged the angels for help and asked them to bind the demons. Suddenly the demon began to resist the invisible hands of his assailants. At once the arms of the demon were in a firm grip, placed behind his back and held there with invisible handcuffs. These were bound so tight that it was impossible to separate the hands, even when we used a stick to pry them apart. The arms suddenly relaxed at the departure of the demon and we could see the marks on the wrists made by the invisible handcuffs. The tying of the demons by the angels took place according to order during every one of the first cases of exorcism. It was also done in some of the later cases.

The angels also tied the feet of the demon round about the ankles. On one occasion the demon was folded together by force as the handcuffs from the wrists were being applied to his feet. With raging madness he decried the angels: "So you wish to pull me together." All these unusual incidents in addition to those signs mentioned in the ritual convinced me of the presence and functions of demons and that we were dealing with genuine cases of possession. The experience of my first three years as exorcist made me acquainted with the conduct and the divisions of the demons. I also became aware of the different phases that a victim of possession passes through before he or she is delivered.

The various phases of possession followed in regular order, and I soon became familiar with the manner in which I was to cope with these peculiar manifestations. There was no further need of any unusual sign for me to diagnose a case of possession correctly. The ordinary facts mentioned in the Ritual and the conduct of the so-called possessed were sufficient for me to determine whether a person was really in the power of demons or not. Later on the unusual signs of possession rarely appeared.

My many experiences afforded me a position similar to that of a medical specialist who has studied the same sickness under different circumstances for many years. The hard earned experience of the specialist enables him to distinguish this sickness from every other similar case. He looks for the characteristic symptoms and, finding them, diagnoses the sickness correctly and is able to predict what the consequences will be. I believe it is exactly that way with reference to the experiences one gets through frequent observation in exorcism. This experience makes it possible to distinguish genuine possession cases from other sicknesses with which in one circumstance they have a similarity.

By experience the exorcist learns to avoid two dangerous mistakes: that of being too credulous and that of not believing at all. The credulous person is tempted to regard all sickness and ills that are either difficult to explain or that are beyond the reach of a doctor, as demoniacal. Many such persons were brought to me as apparently possessed but whom I sent away with the remark that there was not a single indication of genuine possession. The skeptic, following the trend of the enlightened age, closes his mind to all evidence of the nature of possession, because he is under the impression that such things do not happen in our time. He usually regards such cases as being hysterical or neurotic.

Those who will not listen to anything about possession direct their entire attention to external signs or appearances which the possessed has in common with the neurotic and hysterical type. Such signs are certain excitements, deranged movements, deeds of great energy, hallucinations, and the like, but they neglect the evidence of certain signs peculiar to cases of possession which distinguish them from every nervous sickness. Since they form their judgment only from indications of external similarities they conclude that there are no cases of possession. To them everything is imagination, hysteria, nervousness.

The idiot, the drunkard, the lunatic, all gesticulate in a wild fashion. They scream and perform unusual feats. Yet, despite all this external behavior no one would say that the idiot is a drunkard, or that the angry person is drunk or crazy. Why not? Because in addition to these exterior resemblances there are other certain characteristics which distinguish the one case very positively from the other. Such is the case with the possessed. Certain characteristic signs exclude him from the merely nervous type.

I have applied the rite of exorcism to six persons whom doctors had declared hysterical and of the neurotic type. Medical science did not bring about a cure. Doctors had abandoned the cases as hopeless. The exorcism, however, delivered them from the demons, and with the demons all sickly appearances disappeared. One of the possessed still owed her physician a large sum of money. When this doctor saw her fully cured and in the best of health, he was highly astonished.

I knew two young sisters whose external nervousness was of high tension. The mention of God or about the care of souls would bring about this extreme excitement. It was impossible to bring Holy Communion to them. They spent a whole year in a sanitarium where they were subjected to douches and hypnotic treatments weekly. All attempts to put them to sleep in their nervous and excitable condition were in vain. After a year of fruitless attempts they were brought to me.

I was sure I saw in them characteristic signs of genuine possession but as a further proof to convince myself I attempted a short exorcism, treating each individual separately. As soon as I began the prayers of exorcism the young lady lost her consciousness, and the demon made himself known by barking like a dog, and he began to speak to me and to answer my questions.

With this record to support me I can honestly say to the unbeliever: "The exorcisms have healed the sick whom the doctors had declared hysterical and who were considered incurable through medical skill. Either one or the other conclusion follows: either these people were really possessed as the exorcism cured them completely, or the exorcism is the best medicine to cure certain nervous cases which the doctors failed to cure. We call such cases, cases of possession. You, however, are doing them an injustice by depriving them of such a wholesome cure if you do not direct them thither, for you yourself admit that you have no remedy for such ailment."

PART II

The Confessions of Demons

(Preliminary remarks. So far the more general trend of the author shows what a wealth of experience was at his disposal and that he knew how to draw logical conclusions from these facts. We have noticed that he spoke about three kinds of possessions: those who put themselves into the power of Satan through their own fault; others who were innocently placed under the demon's control through curses; finally, certain pious, even saintly souls for whom the possession was an act of atonement, and through which they rescued others from the slavery of sin and from the clutches of Satan. That it is the design of God to permit Satan to exercise such power over pious souls was the conclusion the author drew from numerous admissions that he received from the demons during the process of exorcism. The author assures us that the Blessed Virgin plays an important part in these propitiatory possession cases. This is not difficult to believe, for God said to the serpent: "I will put enmity between thee and the woman, between thy seed and her seed; she will crush thy head and you will lie under her heel." The following chapter deals with these victim souls.)

It was mentioned above that the demon declares himself during the exorcism, and maintains positively that he is a distinct being from the person whose body he controls and sets into motion.

The demon speaks to the exorcist either voluntarily or in reply to questions put to him. God often forces him against his will to confess things that put him to shame. Since the demon is a liar, his own word counts for nothing, especially when he speaks of his own accord. This may happen when the exorcist places useless and curious questions to him. Thus the exorcist exposes himself to the danger of being tricked by the demon's shrewd and evasive answers.

When, however, the exorcist does his duty and places pertinent questions for the success of the exorcism or for the purpose of humiliating the demon, the authority of the Church in the person of the exorcist forces the demon to speak the truth. That is a lesson gained by experience. The Church also presumes that authority since the ritual directs the exorcist in the questions required to wrest the truth from the demon in order to oust him. He is reluctant about answering a question put to him forcibly and will hesitate to reply as long as he can. When he finally yields, one can easily hear his protestations, moans, and repeated pleas: "Must I say this myself? Must it be that way?"

He is forced to speak the truth when he assures the exorcist that he is bidden by the command of God to confess or to make something known. I could give many such examples.

At an exorcism on the 14th of February, 1879, the demon of the possessed was humiliated and on quivering knees pointed out the presence of the Savior and the Blessed Virgin to us. The fear of the demon was most intense. On this occasion he made several confessions. I did not, however, believe him to be trustworthy and said to him: "Are you speaking the truth?"

"Ah," he answered, "if I could tell a lie I would tell you something different."

"And who is forcing you to speak the truth?"

"The very Truth that is here in my presence," was his reply.

I will first state what the demons said about the present state of the Church, and then I will relate the diabolical plans which they, according to their own admission, are keeping under cover.

Since the Pontificate of Pius IX the Church has entered into a period of severe persecutions. The militant Church has to suffer under a twofold evil: externally, through the persecution of her enemies, and interiorly, through the corruption of her members. And since Pius IX ascended the throne, this twofold tendency is constantly increasing. The cause of this heavy burden laid upon the Church is due, according to the confessions of the demons, to the unusually strong and numerous invasion of diabolical spirits upon this earth.

This confession of the demons is confirmed by the prayers after Mass in honor of St. Michael, which Pope Leo XIII has instituted: "And do thou, O prince of the heavenly hosts, by the power of God cast him into hell with the other evil spirits who prowl about the world seeking the destruction of souls." Further testimony to this effect is given by the extended exorcism ritual which the same Pope has issued and sent to all the bishops of the world in order that the authority of the Church might conquer the powers of hell prowling about the world.

The demons plan to harm the Church with every means at their disposal. I reminded Satan during an exorcism that it is not within his power to destroy the Church by quoting: "The gates of hell shall not prevail against her." "We know that," the demon answered coldly, "but we will persecute her as much as it is in our power to do so."

The demons admit that they penetrate everywhere to bring about the ruination of souls, especially through impurity. Everywhere they are spreading "the blackest deceptions". One demon who called himself "Luxuria" and who used the possessed person to imitate femininity, told me proudly: "I have by far more servants than your Virgin (Bl. Virgin) has." They admit that they have won over a large number of souls whom they keep as their slaves and whom they regard as their permanent possessions.

In their battle against the Church the demons use the wicked people as their allies. They have succeeded in enlisting a large number under their banner. "We have the will of the people on our side," they say. The demon "Caesar" leads their forces to stir up governments against the Church. "The people are our trustworthy storm troops" he stated. The Masons are among the main supporters of the demons. Lucifer admits that they are his "dearly beloved children" and calls them "his representatives on earth".

Under the ruse of science, or out of pure curiosity, or simply for the sake of pleasure, people are meddling with occultism and spiritism and make use of hypnotism and engage in every evil practice positively forbidden by the Church. Thus the people put themselves into direct connection with the spirits of the netherworld, and these spirits are none other than demons.

The forces of hell also try to corrupt the priests. The demon who brags about ruining Judas and who parades under that name is planning with his associates to bring about deception, corruption and destruction of priests. Their one aim against priests is to make them traitors. "There always have been such, and there will be such in the future." This demon admitted that he is in charge of all the sacrileges and is the cause of every type of betrayal. It is his aim to seduce priests to carry out his plan. He takes the future into consideration: "There will be many apostates," he said, "and I will use your priests to erect my own church."

He takes great pleasure in dwelling upon the present sad condition of the Church and especially upon the helpless state in which the Church temporarily finds itself. Speaking about Pius IX he said with a mingling of scorn and satisfaction: "You can see in what a nice condition he has left his Church. Look, and behold the power of the Church," he remarked scornfully. "You can recognize her everywhere."

He also spoke with pride and contempt: "You are cowards. Get a move on you! Your God can't even come to your help; you are fainthearted!" Finally he threatened the Church with a bloody persecution: "My slaves will flay your priests as one flays rats," he said.

But after the demons had bragged about their power, their accomplishments, and their haughty plans, they had to make admissions that humbled them and consoled us. They admit that the Blessed Virgin, out of pity for the oppressed Church and in sympathy with the persecuted souls, will come to our aid to break the power of Satan and to cast him and his legions back into hell and thus save the souls now under his tyranny. "She is altogether kind and merciful towards you, but for us she is a torture. She is far worse than her Son," he blurted out. That might be true from Satan's viewpoint because God has given her the power to crush his head. He dared to tempt the Son, but the Virgin Mother, never!

According to the revelations of the demons the Blessed Virgin has selected a little army of noble souls who are prepared to suffer everything and to offer themselves freely to God as a holocaust in atonement for souls. She has selected them to fight directly against the demons. They will break the might of Lucifer's legions upon earth and will deprive him of at least a part of the victims he already counts as his own.

These selected souls will bear up courageously under the attacks of the demons. They will suffer possession in order to free the souls of fellowmen from the yoke of the evil one. They take the place of the guilty to free them from the power of the demon who has darkened their understanding and who is trying to harden their misguided will. It is a worldwide battle between the ferocity of the demon and the victim souls' love for the cross.

The victim souls endure bodily sufferings as well as attacks directed against the sensitive powers of the soul. They will, however, conquer with their spiritual aids. Their lower nature will, so to say, be crushed by demoniacal tortures, but the higher spiritual nature will triumph over the infernal spirits through their generous submission to suffering. Their spiritual powers will increase in proportion to the amount of suffering they endure, for in every loving suffering they will receive an increase of love.

The power of the demons will gradually decrease, at least externally. All their energy will be exhausted in their onslaughts against these victim souls. Should the victim soul persevere in her sacrifice, then her influence will increase, and that of the demon will diminish gradually. Whence it follows that the victim soul will be victorious and the enemy will be completely crushed. The battle between such a victim soul and the demon is a real duel to the death. They are as two gladiators forced to fight until one remains a victim upon the battlefield.

The demon is full of hatred towards all good. "With you everything is love, but with us it is all hatred." He loves the bad only out of hatred for the good. A demon told me that he seduces men to different vices not because he likes these vices but because he despises their virtues. Whenever he sees a virtuous or well-meaning soul whom God might use to accomplish something worthwhile, his hatred becomes inflamed and he tries every possible device to deprive that soul of her virtue and to make her incapable of doing good. He is unable to foretell what the results of his attacks will be for he said to me: "We do not know whither we go." He uses every opportunity to do evil and blindly pursues his hatred against the good without knowing whither his madness and his striving after evil will lead him.

Led by pride he always hopes for success and victory. "I am too proud," he said, "to believe that I will fail in my attempt." Thus he proceeds blindly and to his own shame he is instrumental in bringing about a lot of good. The demon himself told me that there are many things he would not do if he could know beforehand what the outcome would be. All these statements were verified in the actual battle of the demons with their victims.

The demon is aware of these virtuous souls who offer themselves as victims and knows that they are capable of doing much good. Driven by hatred he attacks them without knowing what the consequences will be, but he does not doubt his own success. He gets them into his control in order to corrupt them and to deprive God of their honor. God permits this, but once the demons have freely undertaken to combat these souls, God forces His emissaries to continue the battle to the very end.

The demon will either conquer or be conquered. He said to me: "It seems as if God tells us 'Go ahead, go ahead!' I have to continue." Despite his pride to undertake a battle to a possible victory, he knows and admits that love will win. "Because," he says, "love is more powerful than hatred."

The battle of these victim souls against the demons brings about the very sanctification of these souls. The demon states that a certain number of souls is under the mastery of every demon prowling about the earth. The purpose is not the demoniacal possession itself in the narrow sense, but rather to control the soul through sin and a willing attachment of evil. He regards such souls as his own prizes of spoliation because he beclouds their heart thereby gradually making their return to the good morally impossible. About those souls whose wills have been subjected to his control the demon says: "Whenever I have the will of an individual then I deride your God." Yet he admits that the conversion of that soul is not impossible. "They can repent, but it is very difficult."

Fortunately there are victim souls on hand to wrest these tortured souls from the demon's clutches. If not all, at least a great, number of them are delivered in the following manner:

According to the confessions of the demons, they lose their power in the battle with these victim souls. Not only do they lose the victim, but they themselves are made helpless. They also lose control over the souls that have become their slaves through sin.

After their release these souls for whom the victims have suffered and have made satisfaction to Divine Justice, can again benefit through God's mercy and can easily convert themselves. The devil no longer has any power to prevent them from doing so.

I asked one of the conquered demons who was forced to liberate all the souls whom he kept in the slavery of sin: "Are all these souls converted?" To which he replied: "Some, indeed; the others can be if they want to."

The helpless demons remain in their victims as in a prison, without being able to reconnoiter, or to be externally active. They are awaiting the defeat of their entire band, which is accomplished when their chief is completely overcome. As soon as their leader has lost everything that he and his associates possessed on earth, he has to return to hell, taking all his attendants with him. For the demons said to me: "We cannot remain on earth if we are no longer here in control."

A demon once remarked to me after I had forced him to leave a nun over whom I had performed the ritual of exorcism: "Let me have what I possess on earth and I will leave her at once. But if I have to depart from her, then we must give up everything and return back to hell. For this reason God permits us to defend ourselves to the very last."

The demons maintain that the sins of men give them power over men. They say that God permits demons to keep what they have won through the misdirected will of man, and only the free will of man can take from them what the free will of man has given them. Through the willful suffering of victim souls the demons are deprived of that which men have given them through sin.

During the exorcism of a victim I asked the demon when the sufferings of this victim would cease. He answered that it depended entirely upon the victim herself. She merely had to desire the discontinuance of her suffering and leave the demons in peace instead of battling with them to rob them of these captive souls. "She should remain with her beloved (Jesus)," said the demon of the victim, "and we will let her in peace... Why does she pry into our family? Because she does not want it any other way. It satisfies her." This confession showed that the victim loved to suffer and that through suffering she entered into the realm of the demon and wrested souls from him that he had gained to his side.

According to the constant confessions of the demons it is the Blessed Virgin who leads the suffering souls against the demons and forces them to battle with the victim souls until they are overpowered. The Blessed Virgin ties a host of these to this or that victim. When one horde is made helpless, another one follows to meet the same fate.

That a weak human creature, a victim soul, should ever overpower them humiliates the pride of the demons. "She (Blessed Virgin) should come herself to crush us," shrieked the conquered and humiliated demon, "but to think that two weaklings like yourself and she (the exorcist and the victim) must humble me in such a manner...!"

When the power of the demon is exhausted through rage, he becomes a coward. Courage is a virtue and the demon has no such virtue. Hence he is not courageous but wild, just so long as his energy lasts. As soon as his strength leaves him, he becomes a weakling. "Mercy, mercy! Oh, how I suffer! Enough! Enough! I can't stand it anymore! I am lost! I am miserable! Have pity on me and do not let me suffer so terribly!" Such are the cries of the demon, even the strongest, as soon as he is overpowered.

The demons experience other humiliations, which cause them to become furious with rage. When they torture their victims they make them holy. I have always noticed that these noble souls made rapid strides on the road to perfection. In order to humble the demon I called his attention to the progress of the souls whom he had tormented: "Just look at that soul, how beautiful it is! You have made her so beautiful. When you see her at the last judgment in her grandeur, you can glory in the fact and say 'That is my work!'" This sarcasm caused him to rave. But he continued to battle as long as he had the strength. His pride would not permit him to believe that he would be conquered, nor that he would fail to ruin her soul. "I never permit myself to be discouraged," he said to me. "As long as I have power, I will continue my attacks. I will not retreat."

The demon is especially shamed when one of his previous victims converts, becomes sanctified and finally fights to deprive him of more souls. The young girl mentioned above who, at the age of 11, handed herself over to the devil with a document signed with her blood, became possessed. I exorcised her. The demon was forced to hand over the document which he possessed for 23 years. An invisible hand placed it before us at the end of the exorcism. The demon had tortured this soul fiercely. After having been sufficiently purged by her agony she submitted to the Blessed Virgin's invitation to suffer as a victim to save souls. The demon turned against her in violent revenge: "That is something unheard of!" he screamed. "You ought to know that at one time she was my footstool, and now she snatches souls away from me!"

It is an unbearable torture for the demon to be imprisoned in a victim soul and to be tied to her. The sight of all that is virtuous causes him intense pain, for I have often heard him yell out: "I would rather be in hell than in this filthy person!" Again he said: "Do you think it is a pleasure to be in that morass and to be a witness to all these acts of love?"

The demons often pleaded: "Do let me be free! Let me depart! You have the power to do it! This is truly a glowing oven. Let me depart!" I asked him: "Who has confined you to that person?" "The Virgin," he answered. "Well and good," said I, "if she is the one who has imprisoned you, then it is her affair to free you if she considers it fitting to do so."

The forced union of the demon with another victim caused him to cry out: "If she would only let me go free!" What does all this wailing indicate? "This is a glowing oven! I would rather be in hell than in that house of filth," and similar expressions. This pleading of the demon with the exorcist: "Let me depart! Let her (the victim) free me!" is a proof of the peculiar fact that the demon is made a prisoner in one whom he himself had formerly controlled. He entered the victim soul as a ruler, as a tyrant, in the hope of ruining her. The heroic patience and sincere love of the victim for her mission broke down the power of the demon. After losing the fight he wanted to escape from this humiliating battle. But God commanded him: "Stay there!" And he was forced to continue.

He has to carry on the fight and dare not leave the soul until he is either conqueror or conquered. Being imprisoned in his victim, he can no longer roam about nor harm people just as he pleases.

The imprisoned demon lets out his fury upon the living person like a wild animal confined in a cage trying to wreck it in order to escape. Yet he cannot escape. Indeed, the victim suffers by it but the demon is not freed. By patiently bearing the raving madness of the demon, the victim gradually makes him powerless. The more the demons feel their influence slipping the more furious they become. They admit that themselves: "The weaker we are, the wilder we become."

Besides the people they have won over to their side, the demons also use secret societies as their shock troops. With their help the evil sown by the demons spreads wider and wider like a prairie fire. Despite this help, the demons know the futility of the battle beforehand. They also admit their own defeat and the ultimate failure of the secret societies in their present battle. Their admission on this point is as follows: "We will be cast back into hell but we do not know just when. The hour is determined by your Master, Who is also our Master. Lucifer is not our master; he is our leader." By "Master" they mean God.

God has ordained that there will always be demons upon the earth to try and to test mankind. But the main leaders will have to return to hell and those remaining will be weakened. They will no longer be able to seduce men. The demons told me this themselves. They also told me that once they are defeated, that the time will also come when the members of the secret societies will be humiliated.

The Virgin will destroy the secret societies. "She has already set herself against them." "You will be saved by the Tower of Babel." I presume that by "Tower of Babel" the demon means that all the wicked will attempt an arrogant start that will end to their shame in general confusion, just as the wicked people of the Old Testament attempted to erect the Tower of Babel to make their entrance into heaven.

"The crucified souls are the ones," said the demon, "that will wage war against us." "A faithful soul is more powerful than hell, but a crucified soul is more powerful than a thousand hells." The victim souls will bring peace back into the Church when they have completed their suffering.

The demon "Colerius" spoke about the shameful defeat of hell: "O terrible day! All that we have achieved will be frustrated and what we have destroyed will again be replaced. That will be our greatest disgrace!" The demons likewise announced that heretics and schismatics will return to the unity of the Church in great numbers.

After the most powerful demons will have returned to hell we can well presume that God will enlighten the irreligious and thus lead them back to truth and unity of faith.

When the demon confessed his future downfall I pressed him with further questions: "Then we will share in the mercy of God instead of His revengeful punishment?"

He answered: "Oh, only too true! If it would not be for her (Blessed Virgin) powerful arm...!"

"Is it her arm that stays the arm of God?"

"Certainly, that is the reason why she yearns for victim souls."

"It is therefore her sympathy that longs for them?"

"It is through her that the victim souls get their start."

"The Virgin, then, has suggested the plan?"

"Yes, in her motherly heart," answered the demon.

From these confessions of the demon we may conclude that the Blessed Virgin is selecting noble victim souls who are willing to suffer for love of God. The Blessed Virgin permits them to give battle to the demons that roam about the earth suppressing the Church and ruining souls.

The Blessed Virgin provides a remedy for all our great evils in this manner: She liberates the Church and the souls from the power of these devils; she consoles and placates the heart of her Beloved Son; she makes atonement to God's Justice in place of the sinners and implores God's mercy in their behalf. Finally, she removes from us the avenging justice of God or at least mitigates the punishments. She does not forget those noble souls she enjoins to carry out her plan. They are sanctified through the cross which they have accepted of their own choosing, and through the Blessed Virgin, a reward is prepared for them before God equal to the submission and greatness of their love.

Evidently the aims planned by the Blessed Virgin are of the greatest importance. That makes it intelligible why God should permit these selected souls to be subject to the influence and the actual possession of Satan. The final practical results measured in the scale of the all-mighty and all-powerful God will justify the ordeal of these terrible tests to achieve His ultimate goal. It is true that there will be innocent souls entrusted to the cruelty of the demons. Yet, did not God permit His only begotten Son, Who was innocent and holy, to suffer and die upon the cross in order to deliver the world from the power of Satan and thus bring about the salvation of souls? It was not by His teaching and prayer but by His bitter passion and death that He redeemed us. And did not the Blessed Virgin consent to the sacrifice of her Divine Son, as she stood beneath the Cross? Did she not offer up her sorrows to crush the powers of hell and bring about the salvation of souls?' What she did so heroically for us then through the sacrifice of her Beloved Son, that she continues to do for us now. Despite the sympathy of her motherly heart she sacrifices her loving children, the victim souls, by permitting them to suffer for the benefit of the Church and for the salvation of souls in view of the glorious victory that she will attain over the powers of hell.

That is the program of the Blessed Virgin. What I have said about it is the real truth. It is not a theory fashioned by me, nor a teaching that I would foster, but it deals with a reality which I wish to make known and the veracity of which I believe I can definitely prove. The confessions of the demons prove it; the supernatural revelations give testimony to it.

When I entered upon my career as exorcist I noted down the details of the revelations made after each exorcism. I made a daily note of the supernatural manifestations which took place, during the exorcisms or sometimes in between a series of exorcisms.

I consider myself qualified to give an exact account of the facts as they developed in the course of time without having recourse to my notes. I am able to give the exact words as they have been spoken. All that I mention I have seen and heard myself and have noted it down faithfully during the 25 years of my responsible office of exorcist.

PART III

CORROBORATION FROM HEAVEN

(Preliminary remarks. These occasional confessions of the demons led the Rev. Father to believe with certainty that he understood the meaning of these diabolical tortures to which these pious persons had been subjected. The charismatic graces, speeches, visions, ecstasies, which he regularly observed in these same persons besides the demoniacal influences, confirmed him in his conclusion. To him they were direct proofs that these souls appointed by the Blessed Virgin, through their patient suffering, were making atonement to Divine Justice, were making satisfaction to the Sacred Heart, merited graces for the sinners and helped the Church to gain the victory over the powers of hell. This is the substance of the following lines.)

Besides the certainty of real diabolical influences which could always be observed during the exorcism, there were other indications parallel with those events which, on the contrary, showed positive signs of very unusual divine influences. Among them the following may be enumerated: inner voices, ecstatic visions, ecstasies, heavenly odor, the latter emitted from the victim soul during her suffering or when she was united with God in her ecstasies. All these physically certain facts were testified to by eyewitnesses, except, of course, the interior voices.

Thus I hope to prove that the cause of these graces could originate only from God, that these unusually different influences running parallel with the demoniacal traces can have their origin from God alone.

It does not seem surprising that God on His part should confer such extraordinary sensible graces upon these self-sacrificing souls so dear to Him. He does this to strengthen and to encourage them in their bitter trials since He has permitted the demon to torture them with preternatural visions, appearances, and martyrlike agonies. It would be much more surprising if He would not do it. It would be unreasonable to believe that God, after permitting the demons to crucify these victim souls, would not also on His part extend to them supernatural help. Because, finally, Our Lord certainly is not less noble than the devil is mean.

In order to ascertain with certainty the origin of the supernatural help these victim souls receive, we will have to explain the purpose and usefulness of this divine help.

WHAT IS ITS PURPOSE?

All these very unusual favors have one and the same goal. The interior voice at first invites the victim soul to suffer willingly: "You shall always suffer. Suffering is your destiny. Are you agreed?" The same voice then speaks words of encouragement: "Remain with me wherever my Divine Son wants you to be even at the foot of the Cross. Here all is well."

The voice invites them to suffer for Holy Mother Church, for souls in need and to console the wounded and especially the insulted and offended Eucharistic Heart of Jesus.

This supernatural aid does not deliver the victim soul from suffering, but encourages her to bear up patiently. The interior voice even tells her that her suffering will increase: "The nearer you come to me, the more will I crucify you." And it will also inform the suffering soul that the trial will be painful and will continue for a longer period of time: "The path will be quite long and will be very rough." At the same time the voice speaks words of encouragement: "I am your strength and your shield. Why are you fearful? I am near you. I am the one who suffers, who gives battle, who conquers in your heart."

All the words spoken to the victim souls either through an interior voice or through ecstatic visions have the same purpose. They invite the victim souls to suffer; they encourage them to bear the cross cheerfully; they support them in the battle against the demoniacal powers. This is evidently an exalted and noble aim and it seems impossible that the demon should encourage these souls through supernatural help to fight against him and to rob him of souls. The demon would then be his own opponent.

What, then, are the effects of this supernatural help, or grace? Jesus said: "A bad tree cannot bear good fruit. You can know the tree by the fruit it bears."

So far all these divine favors bestowed upon the victim souls have brought forth decidedly good fruit. In all these victim souls the graces have resulted in a growing love for the cross and a heroic effort to suffer.

I told one victim soul that she should pray for a delay to gain a little rest from her intense suffering. She answered me with touching simplicity: "Dear Father, I cannot ask for that." On her journey to a place of pilgrimage she said to the Blessed Virgin: "My dear Mother, send me no consolations. I ask but for one blessing, the grace always to suffer more and more."

I heard a victim soul say to the demon abusing her: "I have only one passion, the passion to suffer." These noble souls made the following resolution: "To suffer without joy." That is, without any mixture of consolation. In other words, strengthened by grace, they acquire a loving passion for the cross of Christ, and bear their sufferings heroically. It takes a certain amount of heroism to submit lovingly to the fierce attacks of Satan over a period of ten, twenty, and twenty-five years without weakening. The supernatural help strengthens the victim souls so that they not only put up with the demoniacal tortures, but also gladly accept these sufferings which God imposed over and above the pains caused by the devil.

This supernatural help and consolation was not always present. The sufferers were frequently deprived of this aid for a long time. God withdrew and left them to their own sensitive nature. This separation was extremely painful to them, but their former merits and powers received before their suffering, sufficed to help them bear up bravely under these God-given trials as also under the diabolical sufferings. Under this divine guidance not only did their love for the cross become more ardent but all the other virtues were also increased thereby. Especially noteworthy was their perfect submission to the will of God and their readiness to obey His directions during the visions. "My Divine Son needs victim souls who are willing to sacrifice their own freewill."

"You cannot deceive God by offering Him a gift other than the one He wants." Therefore, nothing but perfect, blind obedience is demanded: "Do whatever your Father tells you to do and do not delay long! Follow the directions of your Father and you will not fail. Disobedience cannot be replaced by any other sacrifice."

One completely darkened soul was told that she should follow her spiritual adviser blindly: "Proceed without fear; there is Another Who sees and believes in your soul. Mind the Father and be faithful to Him!"

The love of the cross, the offering of oneself to the will of God, obedience, and all the other virtues, are the fruits which supernatural grace produces in the soul. These fruits are not only good, but very exceptional. Naturally, according to the teaching of the Master, the tree that brings them forth must likewise be very good. In other words, the gifts of grace which have produced such fruits are the workings of the good spirit; they are of divine origin.

The following brief and simple reflection brings us to the same conclusion. It is an established fact testified to by eyewitnesses that the victim souls are influenced by a twofold preternatural influence. These two influences go hand in hand with each other but are of opposite trends and fight against each other. One influence is most certainly diabolic. Physical facts prove this. On the contrary, the opposite influence is divine, just as certainly divine as the other one is diabolical. One needs but see the beautiful expression upon the countenance of a victim soul in ecstasy to convince oneself of its origin. No comparison will do justice to the beaming countenance, the happiness, and the restful peace enjoyed by these souls during that stage. There is nothing more beautiful and soul-stirring than the deep sorrow and tender sympathy glowing in their eyes, the tears that quietly roll down their cheeks when they portray Jesus in His suffering.

The power of the imagination cannot comprehend the depth of these heavenly experiences. The imagination can conjure up the picture of our Lord or of the Blessed Virgin. It can also suppose to hear words, but the picture formed by the imagination and the words that seem to be heard can have no real effect. The picture of the phantasy can bring about transient emotions, but it cannot impart graces to the soul, nor can it strengthen the will to bear the unmentionable sufferings which sometimes last for many years.

I can readily see how a well-balanced person with a good phantasy can, in an overheated imagination and after long and fervent prayer, believe that she truly saw the Master or the Blessed Virgin in a vision. This false vision or illusion has been prepared and is brought about by a previous functioning of the phantasy. But that is not the case in the vision of the victim souls. Towards the end of the exorcism, at the moment when the devil is expelled, the possessed passes immediately from her diabolical condition into the heavenly vision. There was nothing in the victim soul that could have prepared or brought this vision about. During the exorcism this victim soul sat upon an ordinary chair or was reclining upon a carpeted floor. Unconscious and with a diabolical expression upon her face, all her sensitive organs displayed the distorted cravings of the demon possessing her. But upon the departure of the demon the victim passed into the presence of the Master or the Blessed Virgin without having regained the use of her senses.

Nothing could have made an impression upon her senses, her imagination, or her will in a natural manner. She had remained entirely unconscious up to the time the vision appeared. There was nothing present to effect a sudden vision which started the moment the demon had left her. In fact, all the while she had been in the power of the demon, which was up to the time of the appearance of the vision, her sensitive behavior showed a resentful tendency toward the divine.

We can recognize and conclude from the following examples how much the heavenly inspirations help to confirm the diabolical confessions of the victim souls.

It was on March 29, 1876, that I had the first visit from a young lady twenty-nine years of age who possessed a strong will power and unusual intelligence. She was sent by a zealous priest who had heard of me through one of our Fathers. I learned that she had a tender and longing love for the Blessed Virgin although she seemed to be possessed by the devil. To assure myself of her actual possession I observed her for a whole year. My suspicions were confirmed at the end of that time and I asked the Bishop and also my superior for permission to exorcize her. During the exorcism two demons, Asmodeus and Chot, made their appearance and were expelled. The young lady thought she was entirely freed and returned to her home province. A third demon, however, Lucifer by name, had remained hidden in her. As time went on, Lucifer brought the two expelled demons back again together with other demons. After several weeks the condition of the possessed became worse than before. She was brought to me again and I commenced the exorcism with new fervor and with a promising hope.

On this occasion I noticed that besides the unusually diabolical functions there were also extraordinary signs of the divine influences present. In the midst of the diabolical manifestations causing terrible physical and moral sufferings the victim heard the sweet voice of the Blessed Virgin from time to time. This generous and tenderly beloved Mother consoled her, supported her, encouraged her and even reprimanded her at times when she would occasionally permit herself to be discouraged by the horrible sufferings.

In short, the preternatural influences noticed along with the diabolical counterbalanced the latter and gave the young lady power and courage to suffer these unmentionable diabolic tortures patiently for love of God with willingness and resignation. Unknowingly she was being tried and prepared for what Mary had in store for her. The Blessed Virgin did this by instilling in her a great love for suffering and by encouraging her to consecrate herself entirely to the cross of Christ and to a life of suffering.

Here are some of the inspiring words with which the Blessed Virgin encouraged her precious child during the trying moments of possession. On the second day of February, 1878, the Blessed Virgin said to her: "God has prepared a thousand different ways to test your loyalty. Be faithful to Him." On the twentieth of February: "Your heart belongs to me more than ever. I have counted your struggles. If you have an opportunity to pray to me, be fearless, for I am with you. Your trial is not yet at an end. It is still necessary for you to struggle. Renew your vow today and promise that you will always be faithful to me." On February twenty-eighth: "Your place will be near the foot of the cross. The trial you are now to bear will pass over, but you still have some terrible battles before you. I am your Mother. After that you must still suffer, always suffer; that is your contribution. Do you consent?"

The noble child of Mary gave her consent to carry out the plans of her Mother. She was rewarded by being permitted to hear Mary's sweet voice: "I am and will always be your Mother. Always remain with me at the foot of the Cross where my Divine Son wishes you to be. It is well to be here. The cross will fight for you and with you."

On that occasion the courageous soul signed an act of consecration with her own blood. By this act she dedicated herself to the cross of Christ forever. At the end of the consecration she petitioned Jesus for the crown of thorns as a reward for her vow to the cross. The spoken words of the Blessed Virgin had already enkindled a love for the cross in the heart of the possessed, but with this vow to the cross there arose a passionate desire to suffer. Her love for the cross was nourished and increased with every new suffering.

While all this was going on between the possessed and the Blessed Virgin, I continued the process of exorcism during which I was obliged to put up with some awful difficulties caused under Lucifer's personal direction. Until then the divinely mystic influences were noticeable only through the clear and plain words of the Blessed Virgin which the possessed heard in her soul. On April 29, 1878, an unexpected change took place in the presence of the witnesses. At precisely the moment when the demon drew back, the face of the possessed, fiercely distorted up to that time, suddenly assumed a radiant appearance of peace and happiness. It was a joy to see her. Without regaining consciousness and without any transition the possessed suddenly went into an ecstasy. She was favored with a heavenly vision the moment the demons left. Demanding obedience, I asked her what she was seeing. Still in ecstasy she answered in a weak voice that she was seeing her good Mother. I let her enjoy the peace of such a vision that she might listen to the words of her Mother. When she came out of the ecstasy, she told me all that she had seen and heard. She wrote "that she had remained unconscious during the entire exorcism and was not aware of anything that was going on. Suddenly she saw the Blessed Virgin before her."

I will narrate some of the words spoken to her by the Blessed Virgin. Referring to the heart of the Savior Whom she was carrying upon her arms, the Blessed Virgin said: "Look upon my Child and behold the Heart of my Divine Son! From now on have no fear of hell! I will enclose you forever in the Heart of Jesus. I hasten your liberty so that you may spend the month dedicated to me in complete recollection, without worry or annoyance, to whatever heights your obedience directs you."

She was liberated on the 29th of April so that she might use her freedom during the month of Mary and that she might follow the way directed through obedience. I thought it proper to send her to a designated place of pilgrimage, a shrine noted especially for the generosity of the Blessed Virgin, so that she might give thanks to the Mother of Mercy at that place. She spent the month of May without being molested by any diabolical attack.

On the 30th of May, the feast of the Ascension of our Lord, the Blessed Virgin said to her while she was praying before the shrine: "I brought you here to help in the spreading of my name." To which she added: "My Divine Son is in need of victim souls who are eager to sacrifice their own free will." That was the first time the Blessed Virgin spoke about victim souls. The following day the Blessed Virgin renewed the request that she had made the day before: "My Divine Son is in need of victim souls who are eager to sacrifice their own free will." Again she added: "I have selected them from among the weak in order to put those to shame who think themselves strong." In the mind of the Blessed Virgin the plan was there and already arranged. She had already selected the victims who were to participate in it.

Finally, on June 7th, as they were preparing to leave the place of pilgrimage, the Blessed Virgin said: "Travel without fear. You will be one of the first of the victim souls!" Then she gradually revealed more and more of her plans.

Upon her return from the pilgrimage the poor victim was again possessed by the devil and the exorcism began anew. On the 15th of August, towards the end of the exorcism, the Blessed Virgin appeared again, showed the victim soul the Sacred Heart of Jesus and spoke to her: "My dear child, listen to the Sacred Heart of my Son! He has offered Himself for you during the long trials to which you have been subjected. A victim of love Himself, He calls for other victims to offer themselves in atonement for the many insults directed against His Sacred Heart. Are you still hesitating to gain souls for Him?" "The Sacred Heart of my Divine Son is being offended grievously, especially in the Holy Eucharist!" "Take courage, dear child," she added, "you will see me again in heaven, but I will always be with you."

We can see from these pronouncements that this soul was selected to be a victim not only for her own benefit but that she was also to gain other victim souls who in common should render atonement for the offenses against the Sacred Heart of Jesus. The Blessed Virgin did not appear to her again after that. She had promised to remain with her and to encourage her by permitting the victim soul to hear her voice. Thus she spoke to her on the 7th of September: "I expect everything from your obedience and your submission."

On the 17th of September the victim soul, while undergoing terrible suffering, again heard the consoling voice of the Blessed Virgin: "Courage, my child, I am with you. In this way you will win the favor of the Sacred Heart of my Divine Son."

The demon was trying to frustrate the plan of the Blessed Virgin by antagonizing the victim soul against it. To strengthen her will the Blessed Virgin said to her on the 24th of September: "My dear child, your heart was wounded through the Sacred Heart. Take courage, I want you to go to X (place of pilgrimage) and make your perpetual vow there."

Through this consecration the will of the victim soul was to become a permanent vow. From now on she would no longer weaken under the attacks of the evil one. She obeyed the voice of the Blessed Virgin, went to the place of pilgrimage, and made her perpetual vow on the first Friday of the month, October 4, 1878, in the sanctuary of the Blessed Virgin Shrine exactly as the Blessed Virgin had directed her. She was accompanied by two other persons who were ready to consecrate themselves as victim souls with her.

Coincident with the making of the vow before the shrine, a remarkable event occurred at my place of residence. At that time I was exorcising another possessed person who knew nothing about the departure of the former nor about the vow she was to make. During that exorcism in my home town, and moved by a love for the "Mother of Mercy," I requested the demon to depart in her name. It was about twenty minutes past eight o'clock in the morning. The demon replied: "Today is the day of her triumph."

"Did she triumph in her sanctuary?" I asked. "Most assuredly!"

"Whom did she conquer?"

"Lucifer," the demon replied and added: "The holy nuns admire her beauty."

"Whose beauty?" I asked. He did not want to answer my question but said: "Look at the Seraphs! She is sending them."

"Are these Seraphs perhaps the angels of the victim souls?"

After a prolonged protest the demon replied: "Y –e– s!"

Directing myself to the holy angels I said: "You holy Seraphs, bind this demon! Thus I shall know that you are really present!"

The demon shrieked: "Oh, they are terrible!" and he was forced to his knees before Mary, "the Mother of Mercy," whose presence he indicated by pointing to where the Blessed Virgin was situated. Immediately the arms of the demon (possessed person) were seized, placed behind the back and bound tightly together.

Making a record of all these happenings and noting down the words of the demon, I had them signed by the witnesses who were present at the exorcism and sent them to the pastor of the place of pilgrimage. He replied that everything transpired there just as the demon had indicated. Lucifer departed from the victim soul about 8:20 a. m. At the departure of the demon the victim went into an ecstasy. Her companions were very much astonished at how well the demon had described "her beauty" of countenance during her period of ecstasy.

After that the Blessed Virgin said: "I did not call you here for nothing, my child. It was exactly at this spot that Lucifer was to be expelled. Here it is that the insults against my Divine Son shall be atoned for."

Soon after the victim soul had returned from her place of pilgrimage, the diabolical onslaughts began again. She continued her suffering, and I continued the rite of exorcism. The Blessed Virgin no longer appeared as she had previously stated, but the Savior Himself came in her stead. Being assured that the demons could no longer harm her soul, the victim soul felt at ease. "The powers of hell experience no greater satisfaction than to make you suffer," the Blessed Virgin assured her.

The Master appeared to her when the demon was obliged to leave towards the end of the exorcism. It was a rare treat to behold the beautiful countenance, to see the glory radiating from the face of the victim soul as she beheld her Divine Savior. At the sight of Him there was reflected in her face a deep, quiet, loving agony, while tears rolled down her cheeks in great abundance.

Just as His divine Mother had done formerly, so now the Savior Himself called for victim souls: "Oh, my dearly beloved, give the one consolation my offended love desires! Give me hearts that are resigned to accept my mercy and that are ready to acknowledge my tender love! Then you will be a comforter to me." On another occasion Jesus said: "Give me hearts that will share my sorrow and that will sympathize with my bitter sufferings!"

On the 11th of August, 1879, the victim soul saw a wreath of hearts in a vision, and heard the voice of the Blessed Virgin saying: "Behold, dear child, all these hearts will become victim souls. You will have to win them over by suffering in many different ways. Are you ready to do what I ask of you?" The generous soul gladly consented to the wishes of Mary. The Savior encouraged her through His apparitions during her suffering while the Blessed Virgin consoled her with these sweet words: "Be not afraid, dear child. With all this suffering you will gain souls who consider themselves fortunate to offer themselves as victim souls out of love for my Divine Son." And Jesus spoke to her: "Your sufferings bring me joy, as by it you are constantly gaining hearts for me."

It was on November 21st, 1879, that the Blessed Virgin showed her the Sacred Heart in which was a deep wound (not the wound of the lance, but another) and said: "Behold this wound! The Sacred Heart is pained more by the indifference and ungratefulness of good people than by the meanness of the wicked. He is especially being offended in the Sacrament of His Love!"

In December the Blessed Virgin repeated: "The great evils are approaching. The Sacred Heart of my Divine Son is in need of victim souls."

In January, 1882, the Blessed Virgin said: "Dear child, hell has broken out anew with an army. I am anxious to stem the arm of my Divine Son." Then on October 6, 1882, she said: "My loving daughter, behold how the souls really belonging to the Sacred Heart are being cast into hell! You have my sympathy (at that time the girl was suffering severely from the attacks of the demons) but I cannot liberate you. The honor of Jesus and the salvation of souls would thereby be diminished."

In March, 1883, Jesus spoke to the sufferer: "The measure of necessary atonement is not yet sufficient. I would like to be merciful and have compassion on my wicked and ungrateful people..." "Injustice parades about with loftiness and seems to be clothed with authority. Reparations are being made for this anti-God spirit. The time is at hand when the wicked will come out openly. At that very time I will turn their evil plans against themselves and thus destroy their hateful schemes. The Church, for which you are suffering, will gain the victory over them and then she will be more beautiful than ever."

Finally, on September 25, 1883, Jesus encouraged her and informed her in advance that her sufferings will increase according as she becomes more intimately united with Him, and that she will be more sanctified as she attaches herself to the cross: "I am your strength and your shield," Jesus said to her, "Why are you afraid? I am with you, The nearer you approach Me, the more will I crucify you. The path is a long and difficult one; however, after the trial comes, the reward."

These words of Christ have been verified and are becoming more positive from day to day. The sufferings of the victim are constantly increasing, but with it comes also an increase in generosity, steadfastness and heroic love for the cross. (Written in 1901).

A prayer offered by the victim soul in the sanctuary of a shrine dedicated to the Blessed Virgin reveals the heroic disposition of this willing martyr: "My dear Mother, do not send me any consolation. I beseech thee but for one favor, the grace to suffer. Always to suffer more and more." This disposition and prayer fully coincide with the promises of the Savior: "The nearer you approach Me, the more will I crucify you." It also harmonizes with the words the Blessed Virgin spoke to her in the beginning: "You will always have to suffer more. That is your part. Do you consent?'

The appeals I have mentioned clearly prove that the Blessed Virgin is seeking after self-sacrificing souls whom she herself selects. It is through the generous sufferings of the victim souls that the Blessed Virgin seeks to make atonement for the offenses committed against the Sacred Heart of her Divine Son. She thereby wishes to mitigate His anger, to make satisfaction to Divine Justice and thus to obtain grace and mercy for sinners. Her plan is to give constant battle to the demons; to wrest a large number of souls from them and to cast the helpless demons back into hell.

The work of the victim souls is a work of mercy towards sinners as well as a work of atonement and satisfaction for their guilt.

I have no intention to enlarge upon the history of the person so far referred to, nor have I in mind to describe her constant and terrible battles with the powers of hell. I do, however, wish to say this. She has suffered constantly from the time she accepted her mission, and her sufferings are increasing. Countless hordes of demons have passed through her to test their strength against the patience and love for the cross of this soul.

It has been my rare privilege to become acquainted with more than eighteen victim souls selected by the Blessed Virgin. Of these, only two have not persevered. The others were faithful.

The faithful souls are subjected to a twofold influence, one divine and the other diabolical, but in a lesser degree than in the cases of those previously mentioned. I presume there are many others with whom God did not put me in contact.

All the victim souls, scattered over the face of the earth make up "the small fold of victims of the Sacred Heart" as the Blessed Virgin calls them. They have a special mission and are being led along an unusual path. By their generous submission to sufferings they fight and disarm the demons in a sensitively conscious manner. Outside of these, all the "crucified souls" belong to the large army of the Church. The favored group of "Victims of the Sacred Heart" form a select division of the army of the Church.

A crucified soul according to the demon is one who loves the cross and bears it willingly and lovingly. In this instance the cross means that which causes pain to both heart and soul. Such crosses are all spiritual disturbances and darknesses of soul; the feeling of abandonment by God; temptations against faith; temptations against purity leading to discouragement and despair. A soul who accepts these crosses heroically and bears them with love is a crucified soul. She is a soldier in the army of the Church fighting against the powers of hell.

The victims of the Sacred Heart are preferably crucified souls, but, to repeat, one can be a crucified soul without belonging to the favored group selected by the Blessed Virgin, which group is especially prepared by her for battle against the powers of hell.

Accepting the cross with resignation and carrying it with loving attachment is all that is required to be a crucified soul.

Yet, there are many crosses whose burden seems to be too heavy. They bring no merit to souls who bear them reluctantly. But if one should accept them generously and bear them lovingly, then, under no circumstances would they become heavier. Its burden becomes a great advantage and blessing for the specified soul just as much as it would bestow benefits upon the Church at large and also upon other souls in dire need.

Thus far I have referred to the mystic graces in reference only to a single victim soul. God sent these divine helps to her so as to make her campaign against the demons a success. She was to wrest souls from the demons, and finally, after making them powerless, force the demons themselves to return to hell.

Now I wish to mention some of the favors bestowed upon other victim souls. Once I exorcised a very pious young woman, a truly crucified soul. She was possessed by seven devils. At the close of one exorcism at which her husband and other witnesses were present we saw the demon leaving the possessed in the form of yellow smoke. She herself had a vision. She saw the demon in the form of a human being crushed under the foot of the Blessed Virgin. While being crushed, the demon dropped a bunch of keys. At the following exorcism I asked the leader of the demons, who still remained in the possessed person, what the details of the vision were. He explained that the demon who was crushed by the Blessed Virgin was the same one who had been forced to leave it at the last exorcism. I then asked him about the meaning of the keys. He tried to evade the question and it was only after considerable struggle that he finally responded. He explained that "through suffering they will obtain keys which will deprive the demon of the souls he tries to keep imprisoned."

A prominent priest had a victim soul for exorcism and called for me. He wanted me to help him with the rite of exorcism and wrote as follows: "We have here a large number of demons in captivity and some of them are very powerful. Mary is bringing them here. The victim soul is suffering with constant intensity. Jesus and

Mary are strengthening her with powerful graces. She is suffering for the souls consecrated to God and for our country. The demons are approaching in great bands and their leaders are directing their attacks."

The Blessed Virgin ties the infernal spirits in groups to the victim soul in regular order. The demons cannot leave the victim soul. They are enclosed in the victim as if they were locked in a prison. They are forced, to combat with her until one or the other is conquered. The conquered demons are then forced back into hell.

Another victim soul who had to submit to very painful temptations and diabolical visions, especially against holy purity, wrote me: "I begged the Divine Savior to deliver me from this evil. I told him how much I loved holy purity and what an abhorrence I had against the vice of impurity. The Divine Savior consoled me by saying that I am making satisfaction to His Heart through my struggles and was thereby depriving Satan of many souls kept in his captivity through this present common vice. In order to make satisfaction and to soothe the Sacred Heart for these grievous insults there is an absolute need of victim souls."

In conclusion I wish to call attention again to what the Blessed Virgin said to the first victim soul when the latter was a suffering intensely: "O my precious daughter, behold how those who have been blessed by God are being plunged into hell. I sympathize with you, but I cannot liberate you without the honor of my Son and the salvation of souls suffering thereby."

What the demons have confessed is likewise fully confirmed by the revelations made to the victim souls by the Blessed Virgin and our Divine Savior Himself. God permits the victim souls to be attacked and even to be possessed by the demons because He wants the benign plan of the Blessed Virgin to become a reality. The plan is clear and simple.

By means of the free and generous suffering of the victim in battling the demons the Blessed Virgin soothes the wounded loving Heart of her Divine Son. She thereby makes satisfaction to Divine Justice and obtains God's pardon for sinners. By this same plan she saves many souls from the demons who, after having lost their power in battle with the victim souls, are plunged again into the depths of hell.

CONCLUSION

he bitter enemy of Jesus Christ. The Son of Man Whom Satan desperately tried to overthrow has been a stumbling block for him! "I saw Satan descending from heaven like a lightning bolt" (Luke, 10, 8). He swore vengeance against the very idea of the Son of Man and when Christ actually came he persecuted Him with a burning hatred. Those fiends who cried for the blood of Christ, who finally tore His flesh to pieces, tortured His body, pierced His sacred brow, spat upon His face, erected His cross, sealed His grave, were but tools of Satan. Christ conquered Satan, death and hell. The very suffering, the insults and the death upon the cross were the very weapons with which He conquered the enemy.

Christ lives on. He lives in His Church. We are His members. Since his first defeat Satan has sworn greater vengeance against Christ who continues to live in His Church hence, according to the words of St. Peter: "He goeth about like a roaring lion seeking whom he may devour." He who commits sin delivers himself over to the prince of darkness. Satan does not molest the sinner as long as he remains in sin. He flatters him and keeps the sinner in darkness. Should the sinner become uneasy, his anxiety does not come from the evil but from the good spirit. However, he who experiences temptations is made conscious of the new and more powerful attacks of Satan, and those who would become holy would try to be interiorly united with Christ, become Christ-like. They are the living members of the "Mystical Body of Christ," whom the enemy attacks with violent assaults, whom he hates, persecutes, and tortures to the very blood. Should they remain united with Christ and suffer patiently with Him as Christ suffered in the flesh in reparation for sin, then they will likewise become victims of suffering. By their patient suffering they will defeat Satan, and deprive him of souls, and in that way will sanctify their own.

All this is the evident teaching of Christianity. The conclusions of the author of this work are in full agreement with it. I see no possibility of accusing him of error or of credulous deception.

If we take into consideration the present condition of the Church as well as that of the world and of mankind as a whole, we cannot but become serious minded with a troubled conscience. Does Europe still merit the name of Christian? Is it not a known fact that for tens of years past countless parents no longer had their children baptized because they paraded under the banner of the religiously "liberal" minded? Yes, often they had no religion at all. Thus neo-paganism quietly but positively crept into our lives. Today it raises its head aloft and proudly displays its banner. Ten years ago Godfrey Raupert wrote a book, *Christ and the Spirits of Darkness*, in which is written: "I, myself, on the basis of many years of observation and far-reaching experiences, cannot help but come to the conclusion that an untold number of events of our time, many of the inexplicable crimes, the general moral breakdown of human society, the contempt for and the denial of religious truths and laws are, to a great extent, to be attributed to demoniacal influences and machinations. It would be a rather hard task to convince the present world of this and to scare its people out of this sensuality. This world is returning to paganism with giant strides."

I wonder what he would say had he lived to see the battle of the "godless" against religion which Russia is today trying to enkindle and to spread world wide? Is it not plainly the work of Satan against Almighty God? Can it be explained that in the present age of humanism, men who pursue their own fellow men, the harmless, peaceful and noble children of their own country, with fire and sword as is being experienced in Russia, Spain, and Mexico, do it from a pure motive to know, love and serve God? Truly, if Satan does not govern them as once he himself urged the persecutors and murderers of the Son of God, these people could not be so cruel and unjust towards their own comrades! It almost seems that the millennium mentioned in Apocalypse 20, 7, is at hand: "Satan shall be loosed out of his prison, and shall go forth, and seduce the nations, which are over the four quarters of the earth." That is the truth about the great dragon, the old serpent, which will seduce the entire world (Apoc. 12, 9), the murderer of men from the beginning, the liar, the father of lies (John 8, 44). One must be blind not to recognize him by his works.

P. Henry Hurter, S. J., writes in a treatise about possession (Ss. Patrum Opuscula selecta 1, 132): "With the spread of Christianity the dominion of Satan over the world was decreasing more and more and he no longer had the power that he had at the time when man still lived in darkness and in the shadow of death. Now that this love (for Christ) has been chilled, and godlessness has assumed the upper hand over a dwindling faith, need we not be alarmed at the increasing power of the demon? What about these phenomena which were so numerous when the prince of this world was not yet banned... are they not returning?"

Seventy years have passed since Hurter wrote these words. Godlessness is gaining the upper hand.

Ancient paganism was very reverential towards God compared to that of modern heathens. We need not be surprised at the fact that the phenomena insinuated by Hurter, such as diabolical influences upon sensitive nature and men, even to full possession, are evidently being experienced in great numbers again. Many readers may be skeptical on this point because such experiences do not come within their observation and, in recent years, have been tabooed by the press. But the fact remains and there are many testimonials available to prove it. The experiences of such cases have been kept within the limited circle of witnesses for definite reasons. Naturally, those in authority have been informed, but frequently the details of the cases are withheld until they are urgently demanded.

Holy Mother Church has fought unceasingly against the father of lies and deception by spreading the truth through her teaching office, by removing sin and increasing the life of grace through the Holy Priesthood and through the Blood of the Lamb of God upon her altars ascending to the gates of heaven. The Church guides her faithful through the Episcopacy. Would that the faithful would listen to them instead of to the false shepherds in wolves clothing! As a gift of her Divine Master the Church gives to her priests the power to expel devils and to confer blessings. The more violent the attacks of the netherworld, and the more articulate the demons become by their actions, the more diligently should these powers given by the Church be made use of. The exorcist narrates how at one time the Savior reprimanded him for becoming inactive in carrying out the tiresome process of exorcism: "If you love Me, you and the Father, why do you not give more direct battle against my bitterest enemy?" spoke the Master to the victim soul.

The age of enlightenment caused a laxity in the use of the ecclesiastical powers of exorcism through which the bitterest enemy of the Church is contacted. Yet Christ spoke to the Apostles with an authoritative voice: "Drive out the demons." (Mt. 10). It is no longer fashionable to believe that the devil has a direct influence upon the visible world. It is "sufficient" merely to believe in his existence. On page 27, Raupert speaks about spiritualism and mediumship: "It is a pity that in our modern and disappointing attempts to explain the phenomena of mediumship the means of exorcism is not applied as a test, similar to the common practice in the early Christian days. The learned skeptics of today would certainly be surprised at the results."

The history of mankind clearly demonstrates that Satan is in constant warfare fighting for his kingdom, ever urging the wicked against the good, and using the powers of darkness against those of light. Truly Christ came as the more powerful one and has gained the victory over the strong (Luke 11, 22), but His victory was but the beginning. As He was raised upon the cross, His victory seemed to carnal eyes His greatest defeat. This victory must be achieved again by the faithful of Jesus Christ. They are also battling against a mighty power and their greatest victories likewise seem to be their most shameful defeats to the world. Satan is still the Prince of this world and he will maintain his position until the world is converted by fire, that is, by a burning zeal of love through the sacrifice of self. The day will come when Christ's complete victory will be made known to the entire world, and when the prince of this world will be cast into exterior darkness together with his clients. Then the world will be judged (John 12, 31). On that day we will hear the words of the Master: "Depart from Me ye cursed into everlasting fire which has been prepared for the devil and his angels!" (Math. 25, 41). And to the faithful He will say: "Come ye blessed of my Father, take possession of the kingdom which was prepared for you from the foundations of the world." Until the dawn of that day the battle against the infernal powers of hell must continue. Until that day there will be injuries and hardships and blood must flow. However, the final victory is certain and the triumph will be eternal.

Therefore, have courage, my friends!: "Estote fortes in bello et pugnate cum antiquo serpente et accipietis regnum aeternum." "Be brave in battle and fight the ancient serpent and you will gain the eternal kingdom!"

*   *   *   *   *   *   *

We know from revelation that the rebellious angels were cast into hell. Also through the seduction of these fallen angels Adam lost our birthright to heaven. Ever since the fall of our first parents man is conscious that there is something missing. God cursed the earth and everything upon it as a result of man's disobedience to the divine plan. Instead of man ruling the earth, Lucifer and his legions gained the upper hand. The battle is still on. Yet the modern proud type in his overestimated self-confidence does not want to admit that man is in a fallen state. Though God the Father out of pure love for his image, man, permitted His Beloved Son to come upon earth and by His supreme sacrifice upon the cross paid the price to readopt us as sons of God and heirs to His kingdom, we see ungrateful man today flatly ignoring Christ's stupendous condescension. In the U. S. alone out of 120,000,000 there are as yet 70,000,000 not baptized, affiliated with no church. And this despite the injunction of Christ: "Unless a man be born again of water and the Holy Ghost, he cannot enter into the kingdom of God" (John III, 5). "He that believeth not shall be condemned" (Mark XVI, 16). "If he will not hear the Church, let him be to thee as the heathen and publican" (Matt. XVIII, 17). The official medical report tells us that every year in the U. S. 700,000 abortions take place and this despite the injunction: "If thou wilt enter into life keep the Commandments" (Matt. XIX, 17).

Christ gained the victory over the prince of this world, Satan. But man to share in that victory must cooperate with the living mystical Christ. But when the modern world is ignoring, nay even persecuting, Christ, need we be surprised that Satan is coming into his own again and this more boldly within very recent years? The facts contained in this pamphlet should make us more conscious, "That Satan goeth around like a roaring lion seeking whom he may devour." "Watch and pray that you will not enter into temptation." With Christ alone can we gain the victory.

The subtitle: "Sequel to Begone Satan" has been given to this booklet because it helps to clarify the Earling, Iowa, case. Here the supernatural influences were likewise present along with the demoniacal powers. After the exorcism the woman in question immediately passed into the mystic state. She was possessed again later but only for a short time, but ever since she has been a mystic. Thus Father Theophilus informs us: "This person is now rapt in ecstasy at every Holy Mass. At the consecration the Savior appears to her on the cross and bleeding from His wounds so copiously that none of the nails can be seen. During the last four days she has seen Him dying. Gazing at her from the cross with His eyes in which death could be seen, He spoke to her in accents of deepest anguish: 'They condemn My bitter passion and My death on the cross; therefore My crucifixion and death avail them not.' And then He invited her to suffer with Him."

There are many different types of victim souls today only a few of them are possessed by demons. This caution is given so as not to leave the impression that all victim souls belong to this type. Most of them do not. It is estimated that there are over 40,000 victim souls living. The noble example of these heroic souls should spur every Christ-like member on to make atonement with Christ for the sins of mankind so rampant in our day. The more we are conscious that we are brothers and sisters in Christ, all destined to belong to the same family of God, the more active and alive should we also be in the interest of the salvation of souls. If, therefore, the contents of this pamphlet have roused you to new fervor, share it with your fellow brethren. Encourage them to read it: "Whatever you have done to the least of these little ones, you have done unto Me."

A recent very interesting case of possession has come to our attention, namely the case of a 12 year old boy at Rimouski, Que., Can., possessed from 1932-36. The demon took on the form of our Savior to trick this boy for over three years before he was discovered.

May 6, 1936, Cardinal Villeneuve exorcised him at Quebec in his private chapel and the boy has been living in peace ever since.

Pope Leo XIII issued a powerful exorcism formula, an approved copy of which can be had for one cent at the address of the publisher. Exorcism has its full effect only when the priest pronounces it with the authorization of his bishop. To a question directed to the Congregation of Rites the following answer was given, Jan. 7,

1903: "The approbation of the bishop is not necessary when using the exorcism formula as an ordinary approved prayer. Permission is necessary only then when a place or person is to be exorcised by a priest ex officio, when functioning in the capacity of his office of priesthood. In case of need, no priest should hesitate to ask for the authorization."

END

BEGONE SATAN!

A SOUL-STIRRING ACCOUNT OF DIABOLICAL
POSSESSION IN IOWA

AFTER 23 DAYS' BATTLE IN SEPTEMBER, 1928,
DEVIL WAS FORCED TO LEAVE

Written by Fr. Carl Vogl
Translated by Fr. Celestine Kapsner, OSB

IMPRIMATUR: ✠ Most Rev. Jos. F. Busch
Bishop of St. Cloud
July 23, 1935

NIHIL OBSTAT: Rt. Rev. John P. Durham

FOREWORD

In regard to *Begone Satan,* some persons have asked the question: "Why publish a story of this kind in our age and civilization?" One could answer this by replying that our age and civilization needs to learn anew a lesson that was vainly laughed to scorn in past generations.

During His sojourn here on earth Christ cast out devils at various times. The powers of Christ were transmitted to the Apostles and their successors; and the Church's ordinary rite of ordination to the Priesthood includes the order of exorcist, in which Christ's power to cast out devils is transmitted. The Church, moreover, has a special rite for such exorcisms, and throughout the ages she has witnessed the effective use of it. Her long experience also explains her extreme caution, her extensive investigation of a case, before permitting any exorcism.

For a time it was fashionable to scoff at demoniacal possession as part and parcel of an outmoded superstition of bygone ages of ignorance — like the attitude of a lifetime ago in regard to the miracles of Lourdes. But facts are stubborn, also against the scoffings of so-called enlightened criticism. Stubborn facts cannot be denied even when they baffle all natural explanation. The absurd thing about such a position is that the critics "just know" that supernatural or preternatural phenomena simply "cannot be."

We have become much more sober in our day. And it is a healthy sign that the man of education no longer scoffs so readily at that which he cannot explain. So much has been gained for perennial common sense.

To a great extent the essential matters of Christian faith are beyond the field of natural knowledge. However, any viewpoint that is flatly contradicted by true natural knowledge cannot be a matter of Christian faith. In regard to sin and the kingdom of Satan, Christian faith teaches Christ's conquest of Satan and Satan's dominion by His death and resurrection. Now this conquest is shared by individual souls in the sacrament of Baptism, the rite of which contains several solemn exorcisms as well as renunciation of Satan and his pomps. In the light of this Christian faith it is not at all surprising that Satan should be regaining something of his hold on men in our day. For we have in several past centuries witnessed the increased abandonment by men of the Church of Christ, and among non-Catholic denominations the increased abandonment of the sacrament of Baptism. What is this but a great surrender to the powers of evil?

For a succinct statement of the Catholic position on possession by the devil, the reader is referred to the Catholic Encyclopedia, article "Possession, Demoniacal."

Virgil Michel, O. S. B., Ph. D.

BEGONE SATAN!

Nineteen hundred years ago, Christ, the Son of God, came upon this earth. He gained the victory over Satan, the prince of this world, and founded His own Kingdom, the Church. He vested His Church with the same powers that He had received from the Father. "As the Father sent Me, so I send you."

When preparing her candidates for the ministry, Holy Mother Church hands these powers over to them that they may continue the mission of Christ's Kingdom on earth. Preparatory to Holy Priesthood the candidate receives the so-called minor and major orders. Among the minor orders is one called the Order of Exorcist. When the Bishop confers this order he pronounces the following significant words: *You receive also the power to place your hands upon those possessed and through the imposition of the hands, the grace of the Holy Ghost and the words of exorcism you shall drive evil spirits out of the bodies of those so possessed.*

The solemn and powerful meaning attached to this ceremony, not conferred in any of the other orders, can be gleaned from the words: *Receive and impress upon your mind that you receive the right to place your hands upon those possessed.*

Later on the Bishop invites the faithful to join him in asking that he who is to receive this order may be an *effective agent in expelling the evil spirit from those possessed.* He continues to pray that the candidate may become an approved physician of the Church through the gift of healing conferred upon her by the Almighty Himself.

The Church bases her action on the example of Christ Himself, Who frequently drove out evil spirits and endowed His disciples with full authority to do likewise. The superficial faith of our age regards such an order as superfluous. The reality of hell, devils, and cases of possession have been denied as myths of the dark ages. Even if Christ and the Apostles repeatedly emphasized the powers of the evil spirit, these are looked upon as purely superstitious, That Satan has succeeded in making man so indifferent regarding his actions of misleading men is one of the greatest and most advantageous accomplishments. People rarely listen to anything of a supernatural nature.

Actual happenings of the supernatural in our times are all the more striking therefore and cannot so readily be dismissed by a mere shrug of the shoulders — facts such as the numerous and indisputable miracles at Lourdes, the extraordinary visions, stigmata, abstention from food, and gift of languages of Theresa Neumann, the life of the Cure of Ars who was recently proclaimed a saint of the Church, to whom for 35 years the sight of hell was constantly and really an ordinary experience. No less worthy of note are the facts in the cases of possession occurring in our times: the case of a possessed boy in Wemding, Suabia, Bavaria, 1891; the case in St. Michael's Mission in Africa in 1906 of two girls being possessed, one of whom is still living; the noted case of the Chinese woman Lautien in Honan, China, in 1926 and 1929, which was under the direction of Father Peter Heier, S. V. D., of Hague, N. D., now a Missioner in China.

The priest has frequent opportunities for using his power of exorcism. The blessings of holy water, its various uses in the blessing of houses and in the many other blessings and benedictions of the Church in her sacramentals, are dependent upon this power. Pope Leo XIII in our own time has composed a powerful and solemn prayer of exorcism for priests against the fallen angels and evil spirits. It is said that this Pope, after God permitted him to see in a vision the great devastation Satan is carrying on in our times, composed the prayer of exorcism in honor of St. Michael that is now recited in the vernacular as one of the prayers after Mass.

RECENT CASE OF POSSESSION AND EXPULSION IN EARLING, IOWA

The following soul-stirring case of actual possession and successful expulsion, through the powers given to the Church over the evil one, is all the more striking in view of the above explanations. The facts herein narrated are testified to by the Rev. Joseph Steiger, who was a personal witness of the scenes herein narrated. While conducting a mission in the parish of Earling in 1928, Father Theophilus Riesinger, O. M. Cap., asked the Rev. Pastor for permission to have a certain person, whom he believed possessed by the devil, brought into his parish, and to be permitted to use the solemn formula of exorcism over her while she would be detained in the Convent of the Franciscan Sisters who were active in the parish. Father Steiger happened to be a personal friend of Father Theophilus for many years past.

"What, another case of possession?" replied the pastor. "Are these cases still on the increase? You have already dispossessed the devil in a number of such cases!"

"That is indeed true. However, the Bishop has again entrusted this case into my hands. The lady in question lives at some distance from Earling. I should like to have her brought here, since it would create too much excitement in her home and perhaps would be the cause of many disturbances to the person herself."

"But why just here in my own parish?"

"It is just here in an outlying country district that the case may be disposed of in a quiet manner. Two places are available, either in the Sisters' Convent or here in the sacristy. So it is quite possible to relieve the unfortunate person of her burden without anybody out in the world becoming aware of it." "My dear Father, do you really think that the Mother Superior would permit anything like that to take place under her convent roof? I don't believe it. And it would be altogether out of the question to bring the person into my own house."

"My dear friend," smilingly replied the Father, "tell me this one thing. Will you give me your approval, should the Mother Superior be willing?"

"Well, all right, but only under this condition. I do not believe that you will have any success at the convent."

"Thanks for your permission. The case is therefore settled, as the Mother Superior did give her consent from the very beginning. I had already made all arrangements with her for this case provided you would give your full approval."

Thus it was agreed to have the exorcism performed at the convent. The place was situated in the country, and as it was summer time, the people were actively occupied with their work in the open fields. No one would be any the wiser. Much less would anyone bother himself about what was going on.

For safety's sake the case was again submitted to the Bishop, who called the pastor to himself to acquaint him with matters that he might expect to happen.

"So, my Father, you have given your consent to allow this to take place in your parish. Have you thought the matter over sufficiently?"

"Your Lordship, to be honest, I must confess that I was not very anxious to have it. I have a rather strong aversion for such unusual affairs. But Father Theophilus explained that my country parish together with the easy access to the convent would be just suitable for such an undertaking, and so I disliked to refuse."

"As Bishop I will caution you most emphatically that there may be some very serious consequences resulting to you in person. Should the Reverend Father not have enlightened you regarding the matter, then I wish to give you information based upon sound facts and similar experiences. The devil will certainly try his utmost to seek revenge on you, should you be willing that this unfortunate woman be relieved of this terrible oppression."

"Well, I hardly think that it will be as bad as all that. God's protecting hand will not fail me. The devil has no more influence than God permits. And if God will not permit it, the devil will not be able to harm me in the least. So I have no misgivings. I shall keep my word. I have given my consent, and for that very reason I would not care to withdraw it again. And should it entail some sacrifices, I shall be only too glad to bear them if only an immortal soul shall benefit by it and shall be freed from the terrible stranglehold of that infernal being."

The pastor had little suspicion of what the future had in store for him. Today he would hesitate more than once before consenting again so readily. Far be it from him that he should ever live through such experiences again.

THE LADY IN QUESTION

The unfortunate woman was unknown to the pastor. She lived far from Earling, and up to then he had heard nothing about her. The Capuchin Father had explained to him what her actual condition was, that she was a very pious and respectable person now in her fortieth year. Throughout her youth she led a religious, fervent and blameless life. In fact she approached the sacraments frequently. After her fourteenth year some unusual experiences manifested themselves. She wanted to pray, wanted to go to church and as usual receive Holy Communion. But some interior hidden power was interfering with her plans. The situation became worse instead of improving. Words cannot express what she had to suffer. She was actually barred from the consolations of the Church, torn away from them by force. She could not help herself in any way and seemed to be in the clutches of some mysterious power. She was conscious of some sinister inner voices that kept on suggesting most disagreeable things to her. These voices tried their utmost to arouse thoughts of the most shameful type within her, and tried to induce her to do things unmentionable and even to bring her to despair. The poor creature was helpless and secretly was of the opinion that she would become insane. There were times when she felt impelled to shatter her holy water font, when she could have attacked her spiritual adviser and could have suffocated him. Yes, there were thoughts urging her to tear down the very house of God.

"Hallucination, a pure hysterical case, nervous spells." Such easy explanations one will hear to account for the experiences. True, similar happenings do occur in nervous and hysterical cases. However, many doctors had this case in charge for years, and the woman was finally examined by the best specialists in the profession. But their thorough examinations resulted in the unanimous conclusion that the woman in question does not betray the least sign of nervousness, that she is normal in the fullest sense. There was not the slightest indication suggesting physical illness. Her undeniable and unusual experiences could not be accounted for. As the doctors could not help her, it was thought to seek results in another field.

Many years passed. Since the natural means, medical aid and

professional knowledge, were of no avail, recourse was had to the Church and the supernatural powers of the priesthood. But a reserved and skeptical attitude was maintained for some years towards proceeding with exorcism. Examinations and observations were constantly made. However, it gradually became evident that strange preternatural powers were at play. The woman understood languages which she had never heard nor read. When the priest spoke the language of the Church and blessed her in the Latin tongue, she sensed and understood it at once, and at the same time foamed at the mouth and became enraged about it. When he continued in classical Latin, she regained her former ease. She was conscious at once when someone gave her articles sprinkled with holy water or presented her with things secretly blessed, whereas ordinary secular objects would leave her perfectly indifferent.

In short, when after years of trial and observation she reached her fortieth year, the ecclesiastical authorities were finally convinced that here was a clear case of demoniacal possession. The Church must step in and deliver the poor creature from the powers of the evil one. The cause of the possession could not be ascertained. The woman herself could not give any information about this matter. Only later during the process of solemn exorcism was the cause made known.

Father Theophilus had spent many years giving missions in the United States and was familiar with cases of possession. Since he had already dispossessed the evil one in many instances, Holy Mother Church entrusted this case to him. His stainless career, as well as his successful encounter in numerous possessions, singled him out as the one best suited to take hold of this case. He had little suspicion that he would meet with the severest experience as yet encountered by him and that matters of such a nature would confront him as would tax to the limit his physical endurance. Though this Capuchin Father is the very picture of health in his sixtieth year, yet he needed all available resources in order to carry the affair to a successful finish.

The day agreed upon and approved by the Bishop for the exorcism at Earling, Iowa, was at hand. Besides the pastor and his sister, who was his housekeeper, and the Venerable Sisters, not a soul was aware of what was being undertaken. This secrecy had been strictly agreed upon beforehand. The main purpose of such procedure was chiefly to protect the name of the woman, lest anything of the affair might get out among the people and they might point to her and say: "This is the one who was once possessed by the devil." As she was to travel by train, it was found necessary to inform the personnel of the train. For should something happen on the way, their help would have to be available in case the demoniacal influences should create any disturbance. This caution was not in vain, for the men had their hands full. They, however, did not know what the nature of the disturbance really was. The poor creature herself was only too willing to submit to the ecclesiastical procedure, so that she might be delivered from these terrible molestations. Yet she did not always have the necessary control over herself. She made this known after her delivery. Thus, the very night on which she arrived at the Earling station, she was so enraged over those who were to meet her that she felt like taking hold of them and choking them.

Previous arrangements had been made for Father Theophilus to arrive that same night, but by another route. The pastor took his own auto and went to meet him at the depot. Though the new car was always running in tip-top order, it lacked the usual speed on this trip. Everything possible was tried, yet the car would not make any headway towards the station though no flaw could be found with it. The distance was not even worth mentioning, yet it took two hours for the pastor to arrive at the depot. He excused himself to his guest for causing such a delay and disappointment.

To which the latter replied very calmly: "My dear friend, I was not wrought up about it at all. I would have been much more surprised if everything had gone smoothly. Difficulties will arise; they must be expected to arise. The devil will try his utmost to foil our plans. While waiting I prayed constantly that the evil spirit would not be able to harm you, as I suspected that he would try to interfere with your coming, yea, that he would try to injure you personally." Now the pastor understood why his auto had balked. This was to be the beginning of many other unpleasant happenings. After such forebodings the reader can imagine that the missionary entered the car with some misgivings. But he took his precautions. He first blessed the auto with the Sign of the Cross and then seated himself in the rear of the car. During the short ride to the rectory he quietly recited the rosary by himself lest something happen on the way to foil the attempt at exorcism.

The two priests arrived without the slightest trouble. Thank God, the woman also had arrived safely at the Sisters' Convent. With this reassurance the difficult task could begin quietly on the morrow. However, that very night the enemy displayed his true colors. News was soon dispatched from the convent to the rectory next door that the woman caused difficulties from the very start. The well-meaning sister in the kitchen had sprinkled holy water over the food on the tray before she carried the supper to the woman. The devil, however, would not be tricked. The possessed woman was aware at once of the presence of the blessed food and became terribly enraged about it. She purred like a cat, and it was absolutely impossible to make her eat. The blessed food was taken back to the kitchen to be exchanged for unblessed food; otherwise the soup bowls and the plates might have been crashed through the window. It was not possible to trick her with any blessed or consecrated article; the very presence of it would bring about such intense sufferings in her as though her very body were encased in glowing coal.

THE DECISIVE MOMENT HAD ARRIVED

The greater part of the townspeople had gone out into the country to work on their fields on the morrow. All was quiet. Both the pastor and missionary, having offered up Holy Mass in the parish church that morning, went over to the convent where everything in a large room was in readiness for the exorcism. Fortified with the Church's spiritual weapons, they would dislodge Satan from his stronghold in the person of the possessed woman. How long would this process last? It was not to be expected that the devil would leave his victim without a fight. Certainly a few days would pass by before the powers of darkness would give in to the powers of Light, before the devils would let loose the soul redeemed by Christ, and return back to hell. It was well that neither the pastor nor the missionary knew with what kind of horde of evil spirits they would have to do battle.

The woman was placed firmly upon the mattress of an iron bed. Upon the advice of Father Theophilus, her arm-sleeves and her dress were tightly bound so as to prevent any devilish tricks. The strongest nuns were selected to assist her in case anything might happen. There was a suspicion that the devil might attempt attacking the exorcist during the ceremony. Should anything unusual happen, the nuns were to hold the woman quiet upon her bed. Soon after the prescribed prayers of the Church were begun, the woman sank into unconsciousness and remained in that state throughout the period of exorcism. Her eyes were closed up so tightly that no force could open them.

Father Theophilus had hardly begun the formula of exorcism in the name of the Blessed Trinity, in the name of the Father, the Son, and the Holy Ghost, in the name of the Crucified Savior, when a hair-raising scene occurred. With lightning speed the possessed dislodged herself from her bed and from the hands of her guards; and her body, carried through the air, landed high above the door of the room and clung to the wall with a tenacious grip. All present were struck with a trembling fear. Father Theophilus alone kept his peace.

"Pull her down. She must be brought back to her place upon the bed!"

Real force had to be applied to her feet to bring her down from her high position on the wall. The mystery was that she could cling to the wall at all! It was through the powers of the evil spirit, who had taken possession of her body.

Again she was resting upon the mattress. To avoid another such feat, precautions were taken and she was held down tightly with stronger hands.

The exorcism was resumed. The prayers of the Church were continued. Suddenly a loud shrill voice rent the air. The noise in the room sounded as though it were far off, somewhere in a desert. Satan howled as though he had been struck over the head with a club. Like a pack of wild beasts suddenly let loose, the terrifying noises sounded aloud as they came out of the mouth of the possessed woman. Those present were struck with a terrible fear that penetrated the very marrow of their bones.

"Silence, Satan. Keep quiet, you infamous reprobate!"

But he continued to yell and howl as one clubbed and tortured, so that despite the closed windows the noises reverberated throughout the neighborhood.

Awe struck people came running hither and thither: "What is the matter. What is up? Is there someone in the convent being murdered?" Not even a pig stabbed with a butcher knife yells with such shrieking howls as this.

The news travelled through the entire parish like a prairie fire: "At the convent they are trying to drive out the devil from one possessed." Larger and smaller groups were filled with terror as they approached the scene of action and heard with their own ears the unearthly noises and howlings caused by the evil spirits. The weaker members of the crowd were unable to endure the continued rage coming from the underworld. It was even more tense for those actually present at the scene, who with their own eyes and ears were witnesses to what was going on before them. The physical condition of the possessed presented such a gruesome sight, because of the distorted members of her body, that it was unbearable. The sisters, even the pastor, could not endure it long. Occasionally they had to leave the room to recuperate in the fresh air, to gain new strength for further attendance at the horrible ordeal. The most valiant and self-composed was Father Theophilus. He had been accustomed to Satan's howling displays and blusterings from experiences with him in previous exorcisms. God seems to have favored him with special gifts and qualities for facing such ordeals. On such occasions, with the permission of the Bishop, he carried a consecrated Host in a pyx upon his breast in order to safeguard himself against injuries and direct attacks by the evil one. Several times it happened that he was twisted about, trembling like a fluttering leaf in a whirl-wind.

One may ask: Does Satan dare at all to remain in the presence of the All Holy? How can he endure it? Does he not run off like a whipped cur? All we need to remember is that Satan dared to approach our Lord fasting in the desert. He even dared to take the Saviour upon a high pinnacle at Jerusalem; and again he carried Him up on a high mountain top. If he showed himself so powerful then, he has not changed since. On the contrary, the devils living in the possessed displayed various abilities and reactions. Those that hailed from the realm of the fallen angels gave evidence of a greater reserve. They twisted about and howled mournfully in the presence of the Blessed Sacrament, acting like whipped curs who growl and snarl under the pain of the biting lash. Those who were once the active souls of men upon earth and were condemned to hell because of their sinful lives acted differently. They showed themselves bold and fearless, as if they wanted every moment to assail the consecrated Species only to discover that they were powerless. Frothing and spitting and vomiting forth unmentionable excrements from the mouth of the poor creature, they would try to ward off the influence of the exorcist. Apparently they were trying to befoul the consecrated Host in the pyx, but failed in their purpose. It was evidently not granted them to spit upon the All Holy directly. At times they would spout forth torrents of spittle and filth out of the entrails of the helpless woman in order to give vent to their bitter spleen and hatred toward the All Holy One.

You say torrents? Actually those present had to live through some terrible experiences. It was heartrending to see all that came forth from the pitiable creature and often the ordeal was almost unbearable. Outpourings that would fill a pitcher, yes, even a pail, full of the most obnoxious stench were most unnatural. These came in quantities that were humanly speaking impossible to lodge in a normal being. At that the poor creature had eaten scarcely anything for weeks, so that there had been reason to fear she would not survive. At one time the emission was a bowl full of matter resembling vomited macaroni. At another time an even greater measure, having the appearance of sliced and chewed tobacco leaves, was emitted. From ten to twenty times a day this wretched creature was forced to vomit though she had taken at the most only a teaspoonful of water or milk by way of food.

ONE OR MORE DEVILS

During this exorcism it was necessary to find out definitely whether the exorcist had to deal with one or more devils. It was also important for the exorcist to insist upon getting control over the person and of dispossessing the devil. On various occasions there were different voices coming out of the woman which indicated that un-numbered spirits were here involved. There were voices that sounded bestial and most unnatural, uttering an inexpressible grief and hatred that no human could reproduce. Again voices were heard that were quite human, breathing an atmosphere of keen suffering and indicating bitter feelings of disappointment. As is common in such experiences, Satan can, through the solemn exorcism of the Church, be forced to speak and to give answer. And, finally, he can also be forced to speak the truth even though he was the father of lies from the very beginning. Naturally he will try to mislead and to sidetrack the exorcist. It is also common experience that Satan at first does his utmost to sidestep the questions with clever witty evasions, direct lies, shrewd simulations.

When Satan was asked in the Name of Jesus, the crucified Savior, whether there were more spirits involved in the possession of the woman, he did not feign in the least, but boastfully admitted that there were a number of them present. As soon as the name of Jesus was mentioned, he began through the woman to foam and howl like a wild raving animal.

This ugly bellowing and howling took place every day and at times it lasted for hours. At other times it sounded as though a horde of lions and hyenas were let loose, then again as the mewing of cats, the bellowing of cattle and the barking of dogs. A complete uproar of different animal noises would also resound. This was at first so taxing on the nerves of those present that the twelve nuns were forced to take turns at assisting in order to save themselves and to have the necessary strength to continue facing the siege.

The exorcist: "In the name of Jesus and His most Blessed Mother, Mary the Immaculate, who crushed the head of the serpent, tell me the truth. Who is the leader or prince among you? What is your name?"

Devil, barking like the hound of hell: "Beelzebub."

Exorcist: "You call yourself Beelzebub. Are you not Lucifer, the prince of the devils?"

Devil: "No, not the prince, the chieftain, but one of the leaders."

Exorcist: "You were therefore not a human being, but you are one of the fallen angels, who with selfish pride wanted to be like unto God?"

Devil with grinning teeth: "Yes, that is so. Ha, how we hate Him!"

Exorcist: "Why are you called Beelzebub if you are not the prince of the devils?"

Devil: "Enough, my name is Beelzebub."

Exorcist: "From the point of influence and dignity you must rank near Lucifer, or do you hail from the lower choir of angels?"

Devil: "I once belonged to the seraphic choir."

Exorcist: "What would you do, if God made it possible for you to atone for your injustice to Him?"

Demoniacal sneering: "Are you a competent theologian?"

Exorcist: "How long have you been torturing this poor woman?"

Devil: "Since her fourteenth year."

Exorcist: "How dared you enter into that innocent girl and torture her like that?"

Sneeringly: "Ha, did not her own father curse us into her?"

Exorcist: "But why did you, Beelzebub, alone take possession of her? Who gave you that permission?"

Devil: "Don't talk so foolishly. Don't I have to render obedience to Satan?"

Exorcist: "Then you are here at the direction and command of Lucifer?"

Devil: "Well, how could it be otherwise?"

Let it be noted too that Father Theophilus addressed the devil in English, German, and again in Latin. And the devil, Beelzebub, and all the other devils, replied correctly in the very same tongues in which they were addressed. Apparently they would have understood any language spoken today and would have answered in it. Sometimes it happened that Father Theophilus, while in an exhausted state of mind, would make slight mispronunciations in his Latin prayers and words of exorcism. At once Beelzebub would intrude and shriek out: "So and so is right! Dumbbell, you don't know anything!"

Once it happened that Father Theophilus did not catch the words the devil spoke in an inarticulate mumbling voice. So he asked the pastor: "What did he say?" Neither had the pastor understood the devil. Then the nuns were interrogated: "What did he say?"

One answered: "So and so, I think."

Then the devil bellowed and yelped at them: "You, I did not say that. Stick to the truth!"

Father Theophilus indeed was anxious to know why the father had cursed his own daughter. But he only received a curt uncivil reply: "You can ask him himself. Let me in peace for once."

Exorcist: "Is then the father of the woman also present as one of the devils? Since when?"

Devil: "What a foolish question. He has been with us ever since he was damned." A terrible sneering laughter followed full of malicious joy.

Exorcist: "Then I solemnly command in the Name of the Crucified Savior of Nazareth that you present the father of this woman and that he give me answer!"

A deep rough voice announced itself, which had already been noticed alongside the voice of Beelzebub.

Exorcist: "Are you the unfortunate father who has cursed his own child?"

With a defiant roar: "No."

"Who are you then?"

"I am Judas."

"What, Judas! Are you Judas Iscariot, the former Apostle?"

Thereupon followed a horrible, woefully prolonged: "Y-e-s, I am the one." This was howled in the deepest bass voice. It set the whole room a-quivering so that out of pure fright and horror the pastor and some of the nuns ran out. Then followed a disgusting exhibition of spitting and vomiting as if Judas were intending to spit at his Lord and Master with all his might, or as if he had in mind to unloose his inner waste and filth upon Him.

Finally Judas was asked: "What business have you here?"

"To bring her to despair, so that she would commit suicide and hang herself! She must get the rope, she must go to hell!"

"Is it then a fact that everyone that commits suicide goes to hell?"

"Rather not."

"Why not?"

"Ha, we devils are the ones that urge them to commit suicide, to hang themselves, just as I did myself."

"Do you not regret that you have committed such a despicable deed?"

A terrible curse followed: "Let me alone. Don't bother me with your fake god. It was my own fault." Then he kept on raving in a terrible manner.

THE DEMON JACOB

When the prayer of exorcism was renewed, the demon Jacob made his appearance with a healthy manly voice. As in the case of Judas, one could detect at once that he had been a human being.

"Which Jacob are you?" asked the exorcist.

"The father of the possessed girl."

Later developments disclosed the fact that he had led a frightfully coarse and brutal life, a passionately unchaste and debased life. He now admitted that he had repeatedly tried to force his own daughter to commit incest with him. But she had firmly resisted him. Therefore he had cursed her and wished inhumanly that the devils would enter into her and entice her to commit every possible sin against chastity, thereby ruining her, body and soul. He also admitted that he did not die suddenly but that he was permitted to receive the sacrament of Extreme Unction. But this was of no avail because he scoffed at and ridiculed the priest ministering the sacrament to him. Later in the exorcism he made the following explanation: Whatever sins he had committed in this life might still have been forgiven him before death, so that he could have been saved; but the crime of giving his own child to the devils was the thing that finally determined his eternal damnation. Even in hell he was still scheming how to torture and molest his child. Lucifer gladly permitted him to do this. And since he was in his own daughter, he was not, despite all the solemn prayers of the Church, in the least disposed to give her up or leave her.

"But you will obey! The power of Christ and the Blessed Trinity will force you back into the pit of hell where you belong!"

Then followed a loud roar and protest: "No, no, only spare me that!"

As the prayers of exorcism were continued, Jacob's mistress, who was in hell with him, also had to face the ordeal and give answer. Her high pitched voice, almost a falsetto, had already been noticed among the many other voices. She now confessed that she was Mina.

Mina admitted that the cause of her damnation was her prolonged immoral life with Jacob while his wife was still living. But a more specific cause for her eternal woes in hell was her unrepented acts of child murder.

Exorcist: "You committed murder while you were still alive? Whom did you kill?"

Mina, bitterly: "Little ones." Evidently she meant her own children.

Exorcist: "How many did you actually kill?"

Mina, most unwillingly curt: "Three — No, actually four!"

Mina showed herself especially hateful. Her replies were filled with such bitter hatred and spite that they far surpassed all that had happened so far. Her demeanor towards the Blessed Sacrament is beyond description. She would spit and vomit in a most hideous manner so that both Father Theophilus and the pastor had to use handkerchiefs constantly to wipe off the spittle from habit and cassock. Because of her unworthy communions, it was clear that the Blessed Sacrament, the Bread of Eternal Life, which should have been the source of her eternal salvation, turned out to be unto her eternal damnation. For she tried to get at the Blessed Sacrament with a burning vengeance and hatred. Out of this group of devils, Mina and Judas were the worst offenders against the Blessed Sacrament.

The reader would undoubtedly be misled if he were of the opinion that these questions and answers followed in regular order. It must be remembered that these battles and encounters with the devils extended over a number of days. At times the answers were interrupted with hours and hours of howling and yelling which could be brought into submission only by prolonged prayer and persistent exorcism. Often no further answers could be forced from the devils in any other way. Countless brats of devils also interrupted the process of exorcism by their disagreeable and almost unbearable interferences. As a result of these disturbances, the woman's face became so distorted that no one could recognize her features. Then, too, her whole body became so horribly disfigured that the regular contour of her body vanished. Her pale, deathlike and emaciated head, often assuming the size of an inverted water pitcher, became as red as glowing embers. Her eyes protruded out of their sockets, her lips swelled up to proportions equaling the size of hands, and her thin emaciated body was bloated to such enormous size that the pastor and some of the sisters drew back out of fright, thinking that the woman would be torn to pieces and burst asunder. At times her abdominal regions and extremities became as hard as iron and stone. In such instances the weight of her body pressed into the iron bedsteads so that the iron beams of the bed bent to the floor.

According to the prescribed formula of the Church, the solemn exorcism began with the recitation of the Litany of All Saints. All those present knelt and answered the prayers. At first the evil spirits remained peaceful, but when the petitions, "God the Father of heaven", "God the Son Redeemer of the World," "God the Holy Ghost", "Holy Trinity one God," were said, the regular turmoil and gnashing of teeth began. At the petitions, "Holy Mary," "St. Michael," the devils subsided as if struck by a bolt of lightning. A murmuring and muffled groaning arose at the mention of the Choir of Angels and the Holy Apostles. At the words: "From the persecution of the devil," the evil spirit jumped up as if a scourge had hit him. "From the spirit of uncleanliness," how he squirmed! "Through Thy Cross and Passion," how he moaned and yelped like a beaten cur!

ACUTE CAUSE OF THE DEVIL'S PAIN

As the exorcism progressed, one could see that the benediction of the Blessed Sacrament pained the devil most acutely. That was always something unbearable for him. How he spat and vomited! He twisted and raved at the blessing with the Relic of the Cross. Whenever the priest approached him with the cross and the prescribed words, "Look at the wood of the cross! Begone ye powers of hell! The lion of the tribe of Juda shall conquer," he acted terribly.

"Stop it, stop it, I cannot bear it, I cannot listen to it!" he seemed to say.

And when the exorcist approached him with the relic of the cross hidden under his cassock, Satan became a raving maniac. "Begone, begone," he howled, "I cannot bear it. Oh, this is torture! It is unbearable!"

The intercession, "Mary, the Immaculate Conception", caused him fearful agony. When he was addressed, "I command you in the name of the Immaculate Conception, in the name of her who crushed the head of the serpent," he wilted and languished. Then he bloated up the woman's body, and suddenly relaxed as one stunned.

HOLY WATER

Holy Water was also something hateful to Satan. Whenever he was approached with holy water he screamed: "Away, away with it, away with that abominable dirt! Oh, that burns, that scorches!" On one occasion a piece of paper bearing the inscription of a fake Latin prayer was placed on the woman's head. Even the good nuns believed that the prayer was genuine. In reality, the prayer consisted of words taken out of a pagan classic. The nuns were very much surprised that Satan remained so quiet under the experiment. The exorcist, however, knew the cause of the devil's tranquility. Immediately afterwards, a second prepared paper was placed on the head of the woman, which had been blessed beforehand with the sign of the cross and holy water without anybody noticing it. In an instant the piece of paper was torn into a thousand shreds.

LITTLE FLOWER OF THE CHILD JESUS

The pastor had kept a small relic of the Little Flower of the Child Jesus in his sacristy in a small pyx without the knowledge of Father Theophilus. For protection's sake, he placed this in a side-pocket of his cassock one day and entered the convent where the exorcism was taking place. Just as the pastor entered the room, the devil began to rave: "Away, away with that! Away with the relic of the Little Flower, away with that weathercock!"

"We have no relic of the Little Flower," the exorcist exclaimed.

"Certainly, he who just entered has one," said the devil, indicating the pastor. At the same time the pastor approached with the relic. How the devil began to spit and to resist!

At other times the Little Flower played a more important part. One could also notice what a terrific battle Satan had with St. Michael.

ST. MICHAEL

At the very mention of St. Michael Satan began to recoil. He was tortured by that part of the prayer which refers to the solemn petition in behalf of St. Michael. He absolutely refused to listen to the statement that St. Michael, as leader of the faithful angels, cast

Lucifer together with his legions into the very abyss of hell. It was astounding how much he dreaded the prayer in honor of St. Michael commonly recited at the end of the Mass. The prayer is as follows:

"St. Michael the Archangel, defend us in battle. Be our safeguard against the wickedness and destruction of the devil. Restrain him O God, we humbly beseech Thee, and do thou, O Prince of the heavenly host, by the power of God cast him into hell with the other evil spirits, who prowl about the world seeking the ruin of souls. Amen."

Would that we as Christians recited this prayer in honor of St. Michael with greater fervor and devotion.

CRUCIFIX AND RELIC OF THE CROSS

A rather peculiar circumstance induced Pope Leo XIII to compose this powerful prayer. After celebrating Mass one day he was in conference with the Cardinals. Suddenly he sank to the floor. A doctor was summoned and several came at once. There was no sign of any pulse beating, the very life seemed to have ebbed away from the already weakened and aged body. Suddenly he recovered and said: "What a horrible picture I was permitted to see!" He saw what was going to happen in the future, the misleading powers and the ravings of the devils against the Church in all countries. But St. Michael had appeared in the nick of time and cast Satan and his cohorts back into the abyss of hell. Such was the occasion that caused Pope Leo XIII to have this prayer recited over the entire world at the end of the Mass.

As indicated before, Satan dreaded the Sign of the Cross, a crucifix, or a relic of the true cross. On one occasion a crucifix not made of wood was handed to Father Theophilus. This time Satan broke out in a sneering and ridiculing laughter: "Ha, so you arrived with a pasteboard cross! Since when did 'He' die on a paper cross! If my knowledge doesn't fail me, He was nailed to a wooden cross."

The crucifix was examined more closely and was indeed found to be made not of wood but of *papiermaché*. On another occasion Satan made fun of the manner in which Christ was nailed to the cross. "Were not the feet of Jesus nailed one on top of the other, and not aside of each other?" Catherine Emmerich gives the same information. She says that the left foot was nailed first with a shorter nail. Then a longer and stronger nail, at the sight of which our Saviour is said to have shuddered, was driven first through the right foot and then through the left. Those standing nearby at the crucifixion saw very plainly how the nail penetrated both feet.

This does not mean that we are now sure how the feet of our Saviour were placed upon the cross, even if Beelzebub's statement tends to confirm the description given by Catherine Emmerich. We do not give the father of lies credit for being a reliable witness in such matters as the crucifixion even if there is no doubt that many devils were personal witnesses to the crucifixion of Christ. In like manner I would have no one believe that we know for certain that Judas is in hell, just because he appeared in person as one of the damned in the case of possession at Earling. Holy Mother Church has never yet given a decision regarding this matter even though the words of our Saviour about Judas are thought-provoking: "It would have been better if that man had never been born."

As the days passed by, a rather odd experience manifested itself in the disposition of the pastor who began to experience a rather strong antipathy against the whole procedure of driving out the devil.

ANTIPATHY AGAINST THE WHOLE PROCEDURE

The pastor could no longer bear the presence of Father Theophilus who had been a dear friend of his all along, and whom he had known intimately for years. If he would only be out of the way, out of sight! He now wished that he had refused to allow this exorcism to be performed in his parish, and that he had sent him directly out of his house. He became so worked up about it that he finally informed the exorcist of his ill-feeling toward him and the whole affair. Father Th. did not show the least surprise. The case was still in the developing stages and it was only natural to suppose that the devil would have recourse to some source of temptation and annoyance in order to foil all attempts at dislodging him from the one possessed.

Furthermore, the devil used every occasion to display his hatred for the pastor. "You are the cause of the whole affair, you are the one who tortures us so painfully," he burst out. The exorcist commanded Satan on one occasion as follows: "Be quiet, you hellish serpent. Let the pastor in peace once for all. He is not harming you in the least. I am doing this with the powers of exorcism."

This riled the devil all the more. He said: "It is the pastor! He is at fault. Had he not given you permission to use his church and convent, you wouldn't be able to do a thing. And even today you would be helpless against us, if he would retract his assent."

This is an interesting proof of how the devil feels about and recognizes authority. He made this evident to every superior, while he acted rather civilly towards the subordinates. For that reason he never attacked the nuns nor the pastor's cook. All that the pastor or the mother superior had to do was to appear on the scene and the disturbance and raving was on. The mother superior once received such a blow across the face that she was thrust into the corner of the room.

Satan repeatedly threatened Father Steiger, the pastor:

"You will have to suffer for that."

"You can't harm me anyway. I am standing under the protection of Almighty God, and against His power you are absolutely helpless, you detestable hellhound."

"Just wait! I'll make you repent that. I'll incite the whole parish against you and I will calumniate you in such a way that you will no longer be able to defend yourself. Then you will have to pack up and leave in shame and regret."

"If that be the will of God, then God be praised! But you are powerless against Him, you vile serpent, you man killer!"

"Just wait! I will fix both you and your Lord and Master."

"Ha, how dare you speak that way against the Almighty, you despicable worm crawling in the very dust of the earth!"

"No, I cannot harm God directly. But I can touch you and His Church." And he continued with scorn and sarcasm: "Is it not true? Do you not know the history of Mexico? We have prepared a nice mess for Him there."

"Who? You devils?"

"Who else did it? The whole credit is ours for bringing that situation about. He will learn to know us better. Lucifer is on His tracks and will make the kettle hot and heavy for Him. Ha, ha, ha!"

A week later the devil advanced a little closer with his plans of revenge upon the pastor.

"Just wait," he threatened, "until the end of the week! When Friday comes, then..."

The pastor did not take this threat to heart. He was getting sick of listening to the howlings and yelpings of the devil day after day.

Yet the pastor did indeed have a narrow escape on a certain Friday.

THE EXPERIENCE OF HIS LIFE

Friday morning after Mass the telephone rang in the parish house. It was a call from a farmer, whose mother was critically ill. Would the pastor kindly come and administer the last sacraments to the dying? He wanted to call for the pastor with his own car, but somehow it was out of order and he couldn't locate the trouble. He had been trying to start it for over an hour, but in vain. It simply would not start. So he asked the pastor to come with his own auto, or to hire a taxi at the farmer's expense.

Within a quarter of an hour the pastor was on his way to help the sick woman, carrying the Blessed Sacrament with him. After dispensing the last sacraments, Father Steiger was again on the road towards Earling. The road was familiar to him, for he had gone that way hundreds of times, by night and by day, and he knew every bump and stone along the way. He drove very carefully not only because the auto was new, but also because he was mindful of the devil's threats to trick him whenever the opportunity was ripe.

He prayed to his Guardian Angel and to St. Joseph, his Patron Saint, for a safe journey home. Suddenly as he was driving along, a dense black cloud appeared before him. It came just as he was about to pass a bridge over a deep ravine. Great God, it seemed as if his eyes were blindfolded! The next moment there was a crash, a smash-up which dumbfounded him. He found himself in a mess of ruins. The auto had crashed into the railing of the bridge with an indescribable force although he had jerked the car into low gear. The auto, now a complete wreck, was hanging on the iron trellis threatening every moment to drop into the deep abyss below. The noice of the crash was so loud that a farmer ploughing a field some distance away heard the noise and became greatly alarmed. Full of anxiety he hastened to the scene of the accident. Good God, it's the pastor's car! "Father,

Father, what happened? Are you hurt?" The pastor, scared to death, slowly crawled out from underneath the debris. Even the steering wheel was crushed to pieces. His legs would hardly hold him up. The wonder of it was that the rod of the steering wheel had not pierced his breast as frequently happens in such accidents. The farmer hastened home at once and reappeared with his own car. Leaving the wrecked car behind, he took the pastor, still shaking and in a deathlike pallor, into his own car and hurried directly to the nearest doctor to ascertain if there were any internal injuries. No, he was not seriously injured. The doctor discovered some external scars and a state of nervous excitement, but there was no sign of any internal injury. Thank God for that!

Leaving the doctor's office, they drove straight to the parish house at Earling. There was no one at home, for they had all gone over to the convent to witness the exorcism. So the pastor also went there. He had hardly entered the room when he was greeted with a roaring laughter full of vengeance and bitter spleen: "Hahaha— hahaha!" as if the devil were about to burst into a fit of malicious joy at besting him. "Today he pulled in his proud neck and was outpointed! I certainly showed him up today. What about your new auto, that dandy car which was smashed to smithereens? It served you right!"

The others looked wonderingly at the pastor. He was still pale but nothing ailed him otherwise.

"Reverend Pastor, is the devil speaking the truth?" they asked.

"Yes, what he says is true. My auto is a complete wreck. But he was not able to harm me personally."

A quick reply came from the devil: "Our aim was to get you, but somehow our plans were thwarted. It was your powerful Patron Saint who prevented us from harming you."

News of this accident soon spread abroad and the people in deep sympathy with their beloved pastor, collected enough money to buy him a new car, so that the devil would receive no satisfaction from his pranks. Again and again the devil gleefully reminded the pastor of this incident and warned him to "be ready for a whole lot more fun."

The devil also betrayed himself by saying that he is often the cause of similar accidents in order to bring people to quicker ruin.

In that way he can get his revenge and give vent to his anger because lawsuits frequently result as a consequence, which, in turn, are responsible for much hatred and misunderstanding among people.

The reader may make his own conclusions and resolutions regarding this. It cannot be so readily denied that the enemy of mankind actually plays a great part in such accidents. Is he not a "mankiller from the very beginning"? Hence a timely warning to those who use the auto for evil purposes, who decorate it with all sorts of nonsense and who even display figures alluringly immoral. The Church has provided a special blessing under the protection of St. Christopher against evil and disastrous influences. Therefore, it is customary to put one of these blessed medals or medallions in every car for safety's sake. St. Paul calls attention to the fact that the very air is filled with evil spirits.

SATAN'S SPEECHES

It should be noted that Satan did not use the tongue of the poor possessed woman to make himself understood. The helpless creature had been unconscious during the greater part of the trial. Her mouth was closed tight. Even when it was open there was not the slightest movement of the lips, nor were there any changes in the position of the mouth. The evil spirits simply spoke in an audible manner from somewhere within her. Possibly they used some inner organ of the body.

We know from the early Christian writers of the Roman period that the heathens frequently heard voices coming out of their idols. Catherine Emmerich also states that the evil spirits took up their abode in these idols and could clearly be heard to speak from within them in order to confirm the heathens in their delusion of idolatry. So it is conceivable how even some of the highly educated heathens worshipped these statues made by the hands of man, and why they offered sacrifices to them as if they were gods. They rendered to these idols the honor that belongs to God alone.

SATAN'S KNOWLEDGE CAN BE EMBARRASSING

The knowledge Satan had about the sins and the condition of the souls of those present was rather embarrassing to them. But in this case there were no disturbing revelations made along that line as there were only nuns and priests present. But even here he made insinuating remarks: "It is not true that you did so and so in your past life, in your childhood days?" He made reference here to acts which were hardly remembered. The evil spirit, however, would not be quiet and tried to make a scene of things. So the answer was given him: "If before God I am not guilty of greater faults in my later years than the sins of my childhood days, then I am not afraid."

Thereupon followed a most astonishing confession from the devil: "WHAT YOU HAVE ALREADY CONFESSED, I DO NOT KNOW."

What follows from this? Apparently Satan knows only the sins that have not been confessed or repented. What has been submitted to the keys of the confessional seems to be out of his reach. It would seem that the sacrament of penance blots out or obliterates sins from the soul so as not to leave the slightest possibility for Satan to discover them. Through the sacrament of penance everything is, so to say, drowned in the abyss of God's mercy.

The rubrics in the Roman Ritual for exorcism, so wisely and so well established, demand that not only the exorcist, but also all witnesses and all those called upon to aid in subduing the possessed person, should make a thorough general confession, or at least a sincere act of perfect contrition before the process of exorcism begins. Once cleansed from sin they are more at ease in facing Satan and will not be subject to annoying remarks on the part of Satan for the sins committed in the past.

It happened about forty years ago in a case of possession at Wemding, Germany, that during the process of exorcism the mistake was made of calling in the strongest men of the parish, men of good repute, to subdue a raving young boy. These good men did not realize with whom they had to deal. The horrible beastlike howling and yelping was far less disconcerting than the hair-raising reproofs of the devil for the secret sins and other mistakes of one or the other of these men. He described them in minutest detail. Under such circumstances it is not surprising that few people care to be present at such an exorcism, even if they could make themselves useful in many ways. Furthermore, it must be remembered that Satan, the father of lies, often twists small acts into unusually and seemingly grievous ones, making mountains out of molehills, so to speak, and at times purposely distorting them, mixing up truth with falsehood with the intention of creating the greatest disorder and most lasting enmity.

In order to avoid such inconvenient consequences, Father Theophilus, richer by mature experiences, undertakes his exorcism in consecrated or religious houses with only the assistance of priests and nuns. Even then things have happened. Satan shrewdly and sagaciously disclosed hidden things which made certain persons blush for shame; yea, he made them quiver with fear by threatening to expose them still more. All the more fortunate, then, that such experience that will henceforth take place under the seal of secrecy and will not be broadcast to the whole world. Thank God for that!

The meanness of the devil and the many odd happenings at Earling became common knowledge among the people in the bordering communities. The pastor of Earling, Father Steiger, had asked his people to unite in prayer and penance, and to make visits to the Blessed Sacrament so that the evil spirit might soon be mastered. Despite common knowledge of the unusual proceedings going on at the convent, not a single person asked out of curiosity to be permitted to witness the scene. Even if anyone had asked, permission would not have been granted, except to priests from the neighborhood.

It has been intimated above that out of the voices coming from the possessed woman, four different ones could be very clearly distinguished. They announced themselves as Beelzebub, Judas Iscariot, Jacob, the father of the possessed woman, and Mina, Jacob's concubine.

The possessed woman had a clear memory of when her godless father cursed her and handed her over to the devil. She did not mention any further details about her unfortunate father, but it was learned from other sources that he was one of the worst persecutors of priests and of the Church. In sensual lust and excesses he was a monster of the worst type. He kept his distance from the Church and her sacramental ministration, and used every opportunity to ridicule spiritual things. Occasionally, he attended divine services on solemn feast days, but only to acquire new material from the sermons or the solemn functions to feed his ridicule and so bolster up his criticisms among friends and companions. Hence we can understand how he persisted in ridiculing the priest and his actions when, even in his last moments, a merciful God granted him the grace of receiving the last sacrament of Extreme Unction. As you live, so you die. And his concubine, Mina, was fully his equal in this respect. Birds of a feather flock together.

What was most surprising was that such a wicked and blasphemous father was blessed with such a virtuous child. Her sincere piety, her pure and innocent disposition, her diligent application, all were very apparent. Even during the period of possession the devil could not disturb her inner basic disposition because the devil has no power over the free will of a human being.

It was evident that, in addition to the above mentioned devils, there were also a great number of other unclean spirits in her. Among these the so-called dumb devils and avenging spirits made themselves especially prominent.

DUMB DEVILS AND AVENGING SPIRITS

The number of silent devils was countless. Apparently they were from the lower classes, for they displayed no marks of strength or power. Their voices were rather a confusion of sounds from which no definite answers could be distinguished. There was no articulate speech, rather a pitiful moaning and subdued howling. They could put up little resistance against the powerful effects of exorcism. It seemed as though they came and left in hordes, one crowd being relieved by others of the same type. They reminded one of a traveler who is suddenly overtaken by a swarm of mosquitoes. A few puffs of tobacco drive them away, but in short order they return and pester him again.

AVENGING SPIRITS

The avenging spirits were wild and violent, of rough and ill-mannered character. They were filled with hatred and anger against all human beings. Their very presence suggested an ugly and disgusting attitude — a mixture of hatred and envy, meanness and revenge, deception and trickery. These were precisely the ones that threatened to make the pastor rue his consent to this exorcism. They had in mind to stir up the whole parish against him by their misrepresentations, so that he would have to pack up and leave in disgust. One might presume from this that the devils are much to blame for bringing about misunderstandings between the pastor and the people. Not infrequently pastors tell of how they sacrificed themselves, even ruined their health, for the good of the people, but despite all their untiring efforts, some of the most inconceivable misinterpretations and misrepresentations had taken place in their parishes. Some people seem to find it their business to make the life of their shepherd so miserable that he is brought almost to the point of despair. All his good intentions bring him nothing but persecutions of the worst sort. Hence it would not be amiss for pastors to use the small formula of exorcism periodically in order to protect their flocks from such meddlings of the devil, or to use the prayers composed by Pope Leo XIII for just such an emergency.*

The scheming and plotting of these avenging spirits almost succeeded in inciting the pastor of Earling to white heat against Father Th., his friend of long standing, doubtless with the intention of preventing the success of the exorcism. He was so wrought up over the procedure at times that he thought of bringing the whole affair to an abrupt close by driving Father Theophilus from his church and convent with the sharpest words of reproof.

NIGHT PROWLERS

During the process of exorcism, the evil spirits repeatedly made statements to the effect that they would tire and exhaust the pastor. One time in the middle of the night he was suddenly awakened by a disturbance in the room. Were rats gnawing somewhere? It seemed

* See Appendix

to be between the walls near his bed. Was there so much room there that the rats could run about so freely? During his fourteen years in this same house he had never experienced anything of the kind. Was he to be bothered with such miserable pests at last? He pounded the wall with his fist to scare away the rodents. But to no avail. He first used his cane, then his shoe, to pound on the wall. Instead of letting up, the noise became worse. Perhaps the night prowlers would disappear of their own accord. He waited and waited. They continued up and down between the walls, and even threatened to ruin them.

Father Steiger was in need of a good night's rest after all the disturbances during the day. An idea came that seemed altogether too foolish. Could there be some relation between these night prowlers and the evil spirits of the exorcism? Had not the devils threatened to tire him out? Perhaps this is what they meant after all. If so, then there is only one thing to do, and that is to use spiritual weapons against these intruders. Fortifying himself with his stole, the pastor again tried to sleep. At last, the noise let up, but not altogether. "Wait, you cursed hellrats, I'll get rid of you yet!" Getting up again, he lit two candles before a crucifix and recited the small formula of exorcism against evil spirits. Aha! That was the language these hellrats understood. They took to flight and all was quiet. They seemed to have been spirited, blown off now, although all previous thumping and pounding on the walls had brought no results.

A few nights thereafter the pastor again spent a restless night. Are the doors rattling? Is the house quaking? Oh, it's only a heavy express train going through the village, and these noises are only the after rumblings of the jarred earth. The railroad track was only a short distance away. He waited for the train to start from the depot, but he heard no move. Perhaps it's the rattling of machinery in the near-by electric shop!

Finally, the noise ceased. But suddenly it was heard again, this time right above the door. Maybe the door is ajar so that a draft is swaying it back and forth. There was no door stop to catch it, and so he had to get up again. But lo! the door was closed firmly. He took hold of the knob with a firm grip and pulled hard; it did not yield. What, is the devil again at his pranks to tire him out, to rob him of his night's rest? The pastor took the holy water, sprinkled the door, windows, and room, and recited the short formula of exorcism. Again all was quiet. There was not a stir after that. "O you miserable Satan, now I know your stealthly cunning. Just wait, I'll soon teach you good manners."

It was learned later that other priests, who had attended the process of expelling the devil, experienced similar inconveniences and annoyances. Even worse things had happened to them. They would not retire after that without having holy water and the stole with them. The noises were often so persistent that one or the other of the priests was obliged to get up at night and seek the place and cause of the disturbances, and only after praying was he able to find peace again. Night prowlers of this kind have been met with in other cases of exorcism even long after the evil spirits had been driven out of the possessed person.

How the Possessed Woman Fared

Every day the woman lost consciousness and became utterly helpless shortly after the formula of exorcism had begun. When the exercises ceased, she woke up and was herself again. She declared that she was unaware of what transpired during the exercises. Quite exhausted, she had to be carried to and from the place where the exorcism was performed. During all this time she could not eat solid foods, but nourishment in liquid form was injected into her. It was surprising to note how such a weak creature could vomit forth such quantities of material as indicated above. It was not unusual for her to vomit twenty to thirty times a day.

The fact that, in her weakened condition, she could bear up under the daily strain of exorcism for three weeks seems incredible, especially when the terrible abuses upon her body inflicted by the devil are taken into consideration. She suffered so intensely on one occasion that she assumed a death-like color, and seemed ready to pass away at any moment. "Great God, she is dying. I will hasten to get the holy oils!" broke out the pastor, who realized the terrible consequences for all concerned if she died under these conditions. The charge that the priests had caused her death through the strain of exorcism would certainly have been launched against them. Father

Theophilus calmly replied on the basis of his long experience: "Just remain here, my friend; the woman will not die. Absolutely not. This manifestation is only one of Satan's cunning tricks. He cannot and will not be permitted to kill her. Absolutely not."

EXORCISM LASTED TWENTY-THREE DAYS

The period of exorcism extended over an unusually long period of time. Never before did it take so long, as far as we know. It lasted twenty-three days. And remember, the exorcism went on from early morning until late night. The devil tried his utmost to weaken the priests and nuns and to induce them to let up in their untiring efforts. The pastor could not always be present. His care of souls in the parish kept him away at times. Neither was he physically able to sacrifice so many hours of the night for this purpose. Thus it happened that many interesting and also terrible things took place in his absence to which however, the others were trustworthy witnesses.

The solemn formula of exorcism was in progress for more than two weeks before there were any indications that the devil could be forced to depart from the poor helpless possessed woman. Even though Father Theophilus had succeeded in delivering her from a large number of devils through the great powers of the prayers and exorcisms, the four meanest and most persistent ones could not be dislodged for a long time. Satan seemed to have gathered up all the forces of hell to gain a final victory in this case.

HIGH COMMANDER

It was very evident that the forces of hell were under the direction of a high commander who, like a general and field marshall, sent forth new recruits for battle whenever the veterans, in their exhausted condition, were forced to retire. What pitiful sighs and pleadings they sent forth. One could hear voices to this effect: "Oh, what we have to put up with here; it is just terrible, all that we have to suffer." There were other voices that kept on urging their fellow-devils not to let up: "And how we will again have to suffer and cringe under him, how he will torture us again if we return without having accomplished our task." They clearly referred to Lucifer as the torturer.

In order not to give Satan and his hordes any peace whatever, Father Theophilus finally decided to continue the exorcisms himself throughout the night, expecting thereby to achieve his victory. He was blessed with a muscular body and with nerves of steel. He had tested these out by a rigorous and abstemious life of self-denial, which had given him great powers of endurance. And indeed it was something almost superhuman that was demanded of him. For three days and three nights he kept on without any intermission. Even the sisters who alternated were on the verge of a breakdown. Yet the desired effect did not come. It was only with the summoning of his last strength that the exorcist dared to continue. And at the close of the twenty-third day he was completely spent. He had the appearance of a walking corpse, a figure which at any moment might collapse. His own countenance seemed to have aged twenty years during those three weeks.

ANTICHRIST

The reader may at this time be inclined to ask if the devil disclosed things that would be of general interest. For instance, the question of the Antichrist. What did Satan have to say about him?

It must be clearly borne in mind that the questions directed to the devil and the answers given by him were by no means an entertaining dialogue between the evil spirits and the exorcist. On occasions a long time intervened before an answer could be forced out of Satan. For the greater part, only a ghastly bellowing, groaning and howling was the result, whenever he was urged to answer under the powers of exorcism. It was often such a terrible drudgery, so exhaustingly tiresome and irritating, that on some days the exorcist was completely covered with perspiration. He had to make a complete change of attire as often as three to four times a day. Towards the end of those terrible days he became so weak, that he felt he could continue only with the special help of God. Yes, he even pleaded for the grace to be spared his own life. Curious questions not related to the present exorcism were never purposely asked. At times, however, it happened that some of the answers given by the devil himself suggested other questions not strictly pertinent to the case.

On such occasions, Father Theophilus was snubbed by the devil with coarse and harsh replies: "Shut up, that is none of your business!" Satan often used the crisp Latin expression: "Non ad rem!" Which means, "not to the point," "that has nothing to do with this affair."

At one time Satan became rather talkative about the Antichrist. Remember the time he had so triumphantly referred to the Mexican situation, when he said that he would stir up a fine mess for Him (Jesus) and His Church, far more detrimental than hitherto. When asked whether he meant that the furious rage of the Antichrist would be directed against the Church of God, he asserted that that was self-evident and insolently continued: "Yes, Satan is already abroad, and the Antichrist is already born in Palestine. (On another occasion he also mentioned America.) But he is still young. He must first grow up incognito before his power can become known."

In another case of possession the devil gave the years 1952-55 as the time of the Antichrist's appearance.

It is strange that Catherine Emmerich mentioned a similar period, when she gave a description of Christ's descent into hell after His death upon the cross. She related that "when the portals of hell were opened by the angels, there was a terrible uproar, cursing, scolding, howling and moaning. Individual angels were hurling hordes of evil spirits aside. All were commanded to adore Jesus. This caused them the greatest pain. In the center of it all there was a bottomless abyss as black as night. Lucifer was bound in chains and cast into this depth of darkness. All this happened in accordance with set laws. I heard that Lucifer, if I am not mistaken, would again be freed for a time about fifty or sixty years before the year 2000 A. D. A number of other devils would be released somewhat earlier as a punishment and source of temptation to sinful human beings."

On one occasion, when Father Th. insisted that the devil should depart and return to hell, the devil replied in a growling tone: "How can you banish me to hell? I must be free to prepare the way for the Antichrist." And again he spoke out of the possessed woman: "We know a lot. We read the signs of the times. This is the last century. When people will write the year 2000 the end will be at hand."

Whether the "father of lies", as our Lord Himself styles Satan, spoke the truth, it is impossible to judge. At all events, we shall do well if according to our Lord's suggestion, we try to understand the signs of the times. That the powers of hell are putting up a desperate attempt to ruin the Church of Christ in our own times cannot be denied.

* * * * * * *

At one time the evil spirits howled and yelped fearfully when the prayers of exorcism were solemnly pronounced and when the blessings with the relic of the cross and the consecrated Host were given: "Oh, we cannot bear it any longer. We suffer intensely. Do stop it, do stop it! This is many times worse than hell!"

These groans, indicating the attendant pain and suffering, cut to the quick.

"Therefore, depart at once, ye cursed! It is entirely within your power to free yourselves from these sufferings. Let this poor woman in peace! I conjure you in the name of the Almighty God, in the name of the Crucified Jesus of Nazareth, in the name of His purest Mother, the Virgin Mary, in the name of the Archangel Michael!"

"Oh, yes," they groaned, "we are willing. But Lucifer does not let us."

"Tell the truth. Is Lucifer alone the cause of it?"

"No, he alone could not be. God's justice does not permit it as yet, because sufficient atonement has not yet been made for her."

This admission was valuable. It offered a greater inducement to arouse the members of the parish to increase their acts of expiation for the woman.

More Atonement

In accordance with the request of their pastor, the parishioners gladly went to church to keep regular hours of adoration before the Blessed Sacrament. They prayed fervently for the destruction of the powers of Satan, and for the victory of the Church in delivering the victim from the tenacious grip of the devil. Following the directions of the Ritual, the pastor kept on encouraging his people to private fasting and penance in order that their petitions would be more effective in strengthening the prayers of the exorcism. Our Lord Himself, when putting the devil to flight, and after beseeching all to pray, had told the Apostles that this kind of devils can only be driven away by prayers and fasting. The devil's own statement, that sufficient penance had not been done, helped to bring about more fervent prayers and more rigorous penances. The faithful flocked to church in large numbers from early morn until late in the evening in order that, by their prayers, they might add their mite to the work of the Church in this her mission. The exorcism could not continue much longer as the reserve strength of those actually assisting was being vitally sapped.

BATTLES BETWEEN GOOD AND EVIL SPIRITS

It was during this time that the poor woman admitted during her periods of rest that she had visions of horrible battles between the good and evil spirits. Countless numbers of evil spirits continually arrived. Satan tried his utmost not to be outdone this time. The good angels came to assist at the exorcism. Many approached seated on white horses (Apocalypse 19, 15) and, under the leadership of St. Michael, completely routed the infernal serpents and drove the demons back to the abyss of hell.

THE LITTLE FLOWER OF THE CHILD JESUS

The Little Flower of Jesus also appeared to the woman during these crucial days and spoke these consoling words to her: "Do not lose courage! The pastor especially should not give up hope. The end is soon at hand."

This occurred on a certain evening when, to their surprise, the nuns and the pastor's sister suddenly noticed a cluster of white roses on the ceiling. After a while the vision gradually disappeared. The pastor noticed the anxious gaze of these ladies directed towards the ceiling, but he himself did not see the flowers.

The words of encouragement from the Little Flower gave a new impetus to the priests. Now they knew that victory was not far off. During the latter days the devils betrayed great fear lest they be forced to return to hell. Father Th. insisted upon their departure again and again. They pleaded pitifully: "Anything but that, anything but that." To be banished to another place, or into another creature would have been more bearable. They did not want to be driven back to hell.

"But you are already in hell."

"True, true," they groaned, "we drag hell along with us. Yet it is a relief to be permitted to roam about the earth until (at the last judgment) we shall be cast off and damned to hell for eternity."

THE DEVILS DEPART

Gradually the resistance of the devils began to wane. They seemed to become more docile. Their bold, bitter demeanor gave way to more moaning and despairing tones. They could not bear the tortures of exorcism any longer. With great uneasiness they explained that they would finally return to hell. But how often they are deceptive and unreliable! Experience teaches us that at times they pretend to leave the possessed entirely at ease for a while, in order to sidetrack the unwary observer and thus outwit him.

For this reason Father Th., almost completely exhausted, demanded in the name of the Most Blessed Trinity that at their departure the devils should give a sign of their leave-taking from the possessed woman by giving their respective names.

"Are you going to do that?"

"Yes," they promised emphatically.

It was on the twenty-third day of September, 1928, in the evening about nine o'clock that, with a sudden jerk of lightning speed the possessed woman broke from the grip of her protectors and stood erect before them. Only her heels were touching the bed. At first sight it appeared as if she were to be hurled up to the ceiling. "Pull her down! Pull her down!" called the pastor while Father Th. blessed her with the relic of the cross, saying: "Depart ye fiends of hell! Begone Satan, the Lion of Juda reigns!"

At that very moment the stiffness of the woman's body gave way and she fell upon the bed. Then a piercing sound filled the room causing all to tremble vehemently. Voices saying, "Beelzebub, Judas, Jacob, Mina," could be heard. And this was repeated over and over until they faded far away into the distance.

"Beelzebub, — Judas, — Jacob, — Mina." To these words were added: "Hell, — hell, — hell!"

Everyone present was terrified by this gruesome scene. It was the long awaited sign indicating that Satan was forced to leave his victim at last and to return to hell with his associates.

What a happy sight it was that followed: the woman opened her eyes and mouth for the first time, something that had never taken place while the exorcism itself was going on. She displayed a kindly smile as if she wanted to say: "From what a terrible burden have I been freed at last!"

For the first time in twelve years she uttered the most holy name of Jesus with child-like piety: "My Jesus Mercy! Praised be Jesus Christ!"

Tears of joy filled her eyes and those of all in attendance.

Amid the first rejoicings, the witnesses were not aware of the terrible odor that filled the room. All the windows had to be opened. The stench was unearthly, simply unbearable. It was the last souvenir of the infernal devils who had had to abandon their earthly victim.

What a day of joy it was for the whole parish! *Te Deum laudamus!* Holy God we praise Thy name! Not unto us, not unto us, O Lord, but to Thy name be glory and praise!

From that time on the woman, always sincerely good, pious and religious, frequently visited the Blessed Sacrament and assisted at Holy Mass. She received Communion in a most edifying manner. That which was so terrible for her while she was under the torturing powers of Satan is now the peaceful joy of her heart and soul.

THERESA NEUMANN

Theresa Neumann of Konnersreuth was also concerned in this affair.

Bishop Eis of Switzerland, who had been well informed about the above case, paid a visit to Theresa Neumann. And since it was Friday, he asked her while she was in one of her ecstatic visions whether she was aware of the terrible case of demoniacal possession in America. She immediately answered:

"Is it not so? You mean the case in Earling, Iowa, at which some priests scoffed, and about which others were indifferent?"

Then followed an astounding announcement:

"The good woman will later again be possessed. This will be for her own personal benefit, for her own purification and complete atonement."

Furthermore, the stigmatic woman of Konnersreuth had a

terrible vision on the Feast of St. Michael, pertaining to the exorcism that had taken place in Earling. She witnessed the frightful battle between the angels of heaven under the leadership of St. Michael and the infernal demons under the command of Lucifer. She was so shocked and confused by it that she said:

"If it be not against the will of God, I will ask Him never again to permit me to witness anything so terrible."

It was by far the worst vision she had ever experienced.

Father Theophilus, basing his opinion on his numerous experiences with cases of possession, believes that the hour of the Antichrist is not far distant. Lucifer himself was present for about fourteen days in the Earling case. With all the forces of hell at his disposal he tried his utmost to make this a test case. Once Father Th. saw Lucifer standing visibly before him for half an hour — a fiery being in his characteristically demoniac reality. He had a crown on his head and carried a fiery sword in his hand. Beelzebub stood alongside of him. During this time the whole room was filled with flames. Lucifer was cursing and blaspheming in a terrible rage:

"If only I could, I would have choked you long ago. If I only had my former powers, you would soon experience what I could do to you."

Through the powers of Christ he had been deprived of his original might as even now through exorcism his influence was further diminished. Father Th. asked him one time: "What can you accomplish, you helpless Lucifer?"

To which he replied: "What could you do, if you were bound as I am?"

Among the devils who had possessed the woman there were also the four demons that had formerly been tied in the River Euphrates. They had done great harm to the Church in the past. Even today, as Father Th. remarked, persecutions against the Church are significant.

The Earling case brought many priests and bishops to a more serious consciousness of existing conditions. Many of them had been skeptical and made further inquiries. They came in the spirit of the doubting Thomas, but humbly left with deeper faith.

Father Th., who has had nineteen cases of possession under his care within recent years, seems convinced that present indications point to the beginning of a great battle between Christ and Antichrist. He also seems to have learned that Judas will appear as Antichrist in this manner, that a human person, soon after birth, will be controlled and completely ruled by him. Besides the Antichrist, there will be the false prophet, in reality Lucifer, who will perform wonderful deeds and false miracles. He will not be born of a woman, but will construct a body for himself out of earthly matter in order to plot as a man among men. But the faithful need not fear, for all the powers of heaven with its countless angels will be fighting on their side.

END

Rev. Theophilus Riesinger
O.M. Cap.(1868-1941)

Dr. John Dundon,
Physician and Surgeon
1228 E. Brady St., Milwaukee, Wis.

Rev. Celestine Kapsner, O. S. B.
St. John's Abbey Collegeville, Minn.

Dear Father Kapsner:

We wish to indorse your pamphlet "Vade Satana" as a potent aid to faith in the value of sacramentals, relics of the saints, and prayer. No more vivid picture has been presented to us of the losing battle which the great enemy of the human race has been waging against the "camp of Christ". Nothing has made our inconsistent floundering from the "camp of Christ" to the "camp of the devil" appear so absurd. The memory it has instilled of the hatred of Satan and the eternal misery of his permanent army, evokes a continuous inventory of one's life, savoring of the minuteness of the final judgment. That it will save many souls we have no doubt. That some will borrow fruitless fright is also possible, but for them one must say that if the picture is terrible the real thing must be worse. Agony is the lot of all at least once.

Satan has seemed too unreal. It would be a pity if this pamphlet were to be suppressed because some weak souls have been made to sense him more vividly than the author intends.

We were granted an interview with the exorcist, Father Theophilus, after reading your account of the diabolical possession. We treasure the experience as an intimate glimpse into the life of a pious priest very gifted in a specialty which should command the patronage of the medical profession, rather than to be allotted to the realm of superstition or necromancy. We anxiously await his complete report of the Earling case.

Yours very truly,

J. D. Dundon, M. D.

APPENDIX

POPE LEO XIII EXORCISM AGAINST
SATAN AND THE REBELLIOUS ANGELS

Pope Leo XIII recommended that bishops and priests read these exorcisms often in their dioceses and parishes as a simple exorcism to curb the power of the devil and prevent him from doing harm. The faithful also may say it in their own name, for the same purpose, as any approved prayer. (The term "exorcism" does not always denote a solemn exorcism involving a person possessed by the devil, which must only be done by a priest with permission of the Bishop.)

In the Name of the Father and of the Son and of the Holy Spirit, Amen.

Psalm 67:1-2

Let GOD arise and let His enemies be scattered: and let them that hate Him flee from before His Face! As smoke vanisheth, so let them vanish away: as wax melteth before the fire, so let the wicked perish at the Presence of GOD.

Psalm 34:1, 4-9

Judge Thou, O Lord, them that wrong me: overthrow them that fight against me. Let them be confounded and ashamed that seek after my soul. Let them be turned back and be confounded that devise evil against me. Let them become as dust before the wind: and let the Angel of the Lord straighten them. Let their way become dark and slippery: and let the Angel of the Lord pursue them. For without cause they have hidden their net for me unto destruction: without cause they have upbraided my soul. Let the snare which he knoweth not, come upon him: and let the net which he hath hidden, catch him: and into that very snare let him fall. But my soul shall rejoice in the Lord, and shall be delighted in His Salvation . Glory be to the Father, and to the Son, and to the Holy Spirit, as it was in the beginning, is now and ever shall be, world without end, Amen.

PRAYER TO SAINT MICHAEL, THE ARCHANGEL

O Most Glorious Prince of the Heavenly Armies, St. Michael the Archangel, defend us in the battle and in our wrestling against principalities and powers against the rulers of the world of this darkness, against the spirits of wickedness in the high places (Ephes 6:12). Come to the aid of men, whom GOD created incorruptible, and to the Image of His own Likeness He made him (Wis 2:23); and from the tyranny of the devil He bought him at a great price (Cor 7:23). Fight the battles of the Lord today with the Army of the Blessed Angels, as once thou didst fight against lucifer, the leader of pride, and his apostate angels; and they prevailed not: neither was their place found anymore in Heaven. But that great dragon was cast out, the old serpent, who is called the devil and satan, who seduceth the whole world. And he was cast unto the earth, and his angels were thrown down with him (Apoc 12:8-9). Behold, the ancient enemy and murderer strongly raises his head! Transformed into an angel of light, with the entire horde of wicked spirits he goes about everywhere and takes possession of the earth, so that therein he may blot out the Name of GOD and of His Christ and steal away, afflict and ruin into everlasting destruction the souls destined for a Crown of Eternal Glory. On men depraved in mind and corrupt in heart the wicked dragon pours out like a most foul river, the poison of his villainy, a spirit of lying, impiety and blasphemy; and the deadly breath of lust and of all iniquities and vices. Her most crafty enemies have engulfed the Church, the Spouse of the Immaculate Lamb, with sorrows, they have drenched her with wormwood; on all her desirable things they have laid their wicked hands. Where the See of the Blessed Peter and the Chair of Truth have been set up for the light of the gentiles, there they have placed the throne of the abomination of their wickedness, so that, the Pastor having been struck, they may also be able to scatter the flock. Therefore, O thou unconquerable Leader, be present with the people of GOD and against the spiritual wickedness which are bursting in upon them; and bring them the victory. The Holy Church venerates thee as its Guardian and Patron; and it glories in the fact that thou art its Defender against the wicked powers of earth and hell. To thee the Lord has assigned the souls of the redeemed to be placed in Heavenly bliss. Beseech the GOD of Peace to crush satan under our feet, that he may no more be able to hold men captive and to harm the Church. Offer our prayers in the sight of the Most High, so that the mercies of the Lord may quickly come to our aid, that thou mayest seize the dragon, the ancient serpent, who is the devil and satan and that having bound him, thou mayest cast him into the bottomless pit, so that he may no more seduce the nations (Apoc 20:3). Hence confiding in thy protection and guardianship, *by the sacred authority of our ministry* [laypeople omit these italicized words], we confidently and securely begin the task in the Name of Jesus Christ our GOD and Lord, of driving away the attacks of diabolical deceit.

V: Behold the Cross of the Lord, flee away ye hostile forces.
R: The lion of the tribe of Judah, the root of David hath conquered

V: May Thy mercy, O Lord, be upon us.
R: Since we have hoped in Thee.

V: O Lord, hear my prayer.
R: And let my cry come unto Thee.

V: The Lord be with you,
R: And with thy spirit.

LET US PRAY:

O GOD and Father of Our Lord Jesus Christ, we invoke Thy Holy Name, and we humbly implore Thy mercy, that by the intercession of the Mother of GOD Mary Immaculate Ever Virgin, of Blessed Michael the Archangel, of Blessed Joseph the Spouse of the same Blessed Virgin, of the Blessed Apostles Peter and Paul and of all the Saints, Thou wouldst deign to afford us help against satan and all the other unclean spirits and against whatever wanders throughout the world to do harm to the human race and to ruin souls, through the same Christ Our Lord, Amen.

EXORCISM
(Note: the symbol ✠ indicates a blessing to be given if a priest recites the exorcism; if a lay person recites it, they make the Sign of the Cross.)

We exorcize thee, O every unclean spirit, satanic power, infernal invader, wicked legion, assembly and sect; in the Name and by the power of Our Lord Jesus Christ ✠; may thou be snatched away and driven from the Church of GOD and from the souls made to the Image and Likeness of GOD and redeemed by the Precious Blood of the Divine Lamb ✠. Most cunning serpent, thou shalt no more dare to deceive the human race, persecute the Church, torment GOD's elect and sift them as wheat ✠.

The Most High GOD commands thee ✠. He with whom in your great insolence, thou still claimest to be equal; He who wants all men to be saved and to come to the knowledge of the Truth (1 Tim 2:4).

GOD the Father commands thee ✠,

GOD the Son commands thee ✠,

GOD the Holy Spirit commands thee ✠.

The Majesty of Christ, the Eternal Word of GOD made flesh, commands thee ✠; He Who to save our race outdone through thy envy, "humbled himself, becoming obedient even unto death" (Phil 2:8). He who has built His Church on the firm rock and declared that the gates of hell shall never prevail against Her, because He will dwell with Her "all days even to the end of the world" (Mat 28:20).

The Sacred Sign of the Cross commands thee ✠,

As does also the power of the Mysteries of the Christian Faith ✠,

The Glorious Mother of GOD, the Virgin Mary, commands thee ✠; She who by Her humility and from the first moment of Her Immaculate Conception, crushed thy proud head.

The faith of the Holy Apostles Peter and Paul and of the other Apostles command thee ✠.

The Blood of the Martyrs and the pious intercession of all the Saints command thee ✠.

Thus, cursed dragon and thee diabolical legion, we adjure thee by the Living GOD ✠, by the True GOD ✠, by the Holy GOD ✠, by the GOD "who so loved the world that He gave up His Only Son, that every soul believing in Him might not perish but have life everlasting" (John 17:1-3); stop deceiving human creatures and pouring out to them the poison of eternal damnation; stop harming the Church and ensnaring her liberty. BEGONE, satan, inventor and master of all deceit, enemy of man's salvation. Give place to Christ in whom thou hast found none of your works; give place to the One,

Holy, Catholic and Apostolic Church acquired by Christ at the price of His Blood. Stoop beneath the powerful Hand of GOD; tremble and flee when we invoke the Holy and terrible Name of Jesus, this Name which causes hell to tremble, this Name to which the Virtues, Powers and Dominations of Heaven are humbly submissive, this Name which the Cherubim and Seraphim praise unceasingly repeating: Holy, Holy, Holy is the Lord, the GOD of Hosts!

V: O Lord, hear my prayer,
R: And let my cry come unto Thee

V: May the Lord be with thee,
R: And with thy spirit.

LET US PRAY:

GOD of Heaven, GOD of Earth, GOD of Angels, GOD of Archangels, GOD of Patriarchs, GOD of Prophets, GOD of Apostles, GOD of Martyrs, GOD of Confessors, GOD of Virgins, GOD Who has power to give life after death and rest after work, because there is no other GOD than Thee and there can be no other, for Thou art the Creator of all things, visible and invisible, of whose Reign there shall be no end. We humbly prostrate ourselves before Thy Glorious Majesty and we beseech Thee to deliver us by Thy Power from all the tyranny of the infernal spirits, from their snares, their lies and their furious wickedness; deign, O Lord, to grant us Thy powerful protection and to keep us safe and sound. We beseech Thee through Jesus Christ Our Lord, Amen.

V: From the snares of the devil,
R: Deliver us O Lord.

V: Grant that Thy Church may serve Thee in secure liberty,
R: We beseech Thee, hear us.

V: Deign to crush down the enemies of the Holy Church,
R: We beseech Thee, hear us.

Holy Water is sprinkled.

PRAYER FOR DELIVERANCE

Lord Jesus Christ,
after calming the storms and freeing the possessed
you gave us a sign of your mercy in assigning
   the power to overcome evil spirits to your Church.
We pray for your servant.
Hold in check the power of the evil one,
and show him (her) your mercy;
heal in him (her) the wounds of sin
and fill him (her) heart with your peace.
I command you, Satan, enemy of man's salvation,
acknowledge the power and might of Jesus Christ
who conquered you in the wilderness,
overcame you in the garden,
robbed you of your prey upon the Cross
and by rising from the tomb
bore off your prize to the kingdom of light:
depart from N. whom God has created,
whom Jesus Christ won for Himself by His own Blood,
leave forever this man (woman)
whom God has anointed to be a holy temple
   of his Holy Spirit.
Go therefore Satan and never return, in the name
of the Father ✠ and of the Son h
   and of the Holy ✠ Spirit;
go through the faith and the prayer of the Church;
go through the sign of the holy ✠ Cross
   of Jesus Christ our Lord
who lives and reigns forever and ever. Amen.

PRAYER FOR INNER HEALING

Lord Jesus, you came to heal our wounded and troubled hearts. I beg you to heal the torments that cause anxiety in my heart. I beg you, in a particular way, to heal all who are the cause of sin. I beg you to come into my life and heal me of the psychological harms that struck me in my early years and from the injuries that they caused throughout my life.

Lord Jesus, you know my burdens. I lay them all on your Good Shepherd's heart. I beseech you - by the merits of the great, open wound in your heart - to heal the small wounds that are in mine. Heal the pain of my memories, so that nothing that has happened to me will cause me to remain in pain and anguish, filled with anxiety.

Heal, O Lord, all those wounds that have been the cause of the evil that is rooted in my life. I want to forgive all those who have offended me. Look to those inner sores that make me unable to forgive. You who came to forgive the afflicted of heart, please, heal my own heart. Heal, my Lord Jesus, those intimate wounds that cause me physical illness. I offer you my heart, accept it, Lord, purify it and give me the sentiments of your Divine Heart. Help me to be meek and humble.

Heal me, O Lord, from the pain caused by the death of my loved ones, which is oppressing me. Grant me to regain peace and joy in the knowledge that you are the Resurrection and the Life. Make me an authentic witness to your resurrection, your victory over sin and death, your living presence among us. Amen.

PRAYER FOR PROTECTION AND DELIVERANCE

Heavenly Father, I praise and thank you for all you have given me. Please cover me with the protective, precious blood of your Son, Jesus Christ, and increase your Holy Spirit in me with His gifts of wisdom, knowledge, understanding, hunger for prayer, guidance and discernment to help me know your will and surrender to it more completely.

Father please heal my negative emotions and any wounds in my heart and spirit. Send the sword of your Holy Spirit to sever and break all spells, curses, hexes, voodoo and all negative genetic, inter-generational and addictive material, past, present or to come, known or unknown, against me, my relationships and family, finances, possessions and ministry.

Father I forgive and I ask forgiveness for my sins and failings and I ask that my whole person, body and mind, heart and will, soul and spirit, memory and emotions, attitudes and values lie cleansed, renewed and protected by the most precious Blood of your Son Jesus.

In the Name, power, Blood and authority of Jesus Christ I bind and break the power and effect in or around me of any and all evil spirits who are trying to harm me in any way and I command these spirits and their companion spirits in the name of the Father, the Son and the Holy Spirit to leave me peacefully and quietly and go immediately and directly to the Eucharistic Presence of Jesus Christ in the closest Catholic Church tabernacle, to be disposed of by Jesus and never again to harm me.

Dear Holy Spirit please fill up any void in me to overflowing with your great love. All this, Father, I pray in the Name of Jesus Christ by the guidance of your Holy Spirit. Immaculate Heart of Mary, spouse of the Holy Spirit, please pray for me and with me. Amen.

Made in the USA
Middletown, DE
27 January 2020